SHADOW WORK DEEP DIVE JOURNAL

A GUIDE TO STEP INTO YOUR AUTHENTIC SELF, HEAL YOUR INNER CHILD & INTEGRATE YOUR SHADOW

ABSTRACT THOUGHTS

CONTENTS

INTRODUCTION

Have you ever encountered a version of yourself that took you by surprise—an unexplained and uncharacteristic reaction to something, or a flicker in your eye in the mirror that hinted at emotions you weren't aware you were harboring? What if I told you these moments are mere glimpses into a vast, unexplored landscape within you? A place filled with forgotten memories, suppressed emotions, and untapped potential. Welcome to the world of shadow work—a transformative journey inward, one that promises not only self-discovery but also self-mastery.

This book is your personal guide to one of the most transformative psychological practices: shadow work. Coined by the pioneering psychologist Carl Jung, the concept of the 'shadow self' refers to the hidden parts of us that reside in the unconscious—a mosaic of desires, fears, and capacities we don't acknowledge or can't see. It's all that we've pushed out of our awareness because it made us uncomfortable or didn't fit our self-image. But here's the kicker: Your shadow is not your enemy. It's a part of you that's crying out for attention, understanding, and integration. And by doing so, can allow you to heal past trauma, experience immense personal growth and ultimately step into your most authentic self.

This guide is for you if you're tired of being haunted by past traumas, confusing emotions, and unexplained reactions that seem to govern your life. It's for you if you've ever felt that there's more to you than meets the eye, and you're yearning to untangle the intricate web of your mind and soul. It's for all those who wish to live a life not dictated by hidden fears or suppressed desires but guided by wholeness, acceptance, and, above all, profound self-love.

So whether you're new to the concept of shadow work or have dabbled in it before but felt overwhelmed, this book offers a structured yet flexible approach that will help you navigate your inner world. This isn't just a theoretical treatise; it's a practical workbook filled with exercises, prompts, and guided reflections that will serve as your map on this intricate journey.

In this all-encompassing guide, we'll start in Section 1 by introducing you to the rich psychological framework woven by Carl Jung, helping you contextualize your own shadow work journey within broader psychological paradigms. From there moving into Section 2, we'll dive into the complexities of your own mind, differentiating between the conscious and unconscious realms, and understanding the role of your ego in shaping your experiences. This isn't just theory; it's punctuated with hands-on exercises and introspective prompts that serve as your first steps into this intricate terrain.

Next, when we get to Section 3 we'll cover the nuts and bolts of how to actually engage in shadow work, equipping you with practical tools and strategies to get started and face any challenges head-on.

You'll find that self-compassion is a cornerstone in this transformative work, providing a buffer against the negative self-judgment that can often arise. As we dig deeper, we'll explore techniques to keep yourself grounded, both emotionally and psychologically, before and after engaging with your shadow. Learning to spot signs and triggers that indicate your shadow is vying for attention will come next once we transition to Section 4, followed by actionable steps to accept, love, and integrate these previously hidden or rejected parts into your conscious awareness. The book also dives into the complex landscape of your emotions, shedding new light on feelings as both triggers and gateways to deeper understanding of your shadow. Finally, we culminate with a variety of hands-on shadow work exercises, like Wounding Mapping, Fill in the Blanks, Inner Child Affirmations, and Gratitude Lists, all designed to provide practical steps for deep inner work.

Embarking on this journey requires courage and an open mind, but the rewards are immense. You'll find yourself not only healing past wounds but also making room for new growth, deeper connections, and a life that resonates with your truest self.

So, are you ready to delve into the mysterious depths of your own psyche, face your shadow, and emerge not just enlightened but also whole? Open this book, and let's begin your transformative journey.

Welcome to your uncharted terrain. Welcome to the world of shadow work.

SECTION 1

THE SHADOW UNVEILED

Journeying inward isn't for the faint of heart. Much like an intrepid explorer charting unknown terrains, we're about to embark on an odyssey—an internal one. The goal? To illuminate the dark, unexplored recesses of our own minds. And who better to guide us than the pioneer Carl Jung?

Jung's life unfolds like a meticulously detailed map of the human psyche. Born in Switzerland in 1875, he grew up not just witnessing but actively shaping the ebbs and flows of psychological thought. His explorations took him to depths that many wouldn't dare venture into, even diving into areas where his contemporaries, including Freud, feared to tread.

In his early life, Jung once carved a mannequin and secreted it away in the attic—a simple, covert act that spoke volumes. This, dear reader, serves as our compass. That hidden figure, tucked away, mirrors the shadows within us, urging us to dig deeper, to seek out the parts of us that lie concealed, waiting to be acknowledged.

So, as we stand at the threshold, take a moment to breathe. Whether you're here to heal a wounded inner child, release blocked energy, or simply delve into your own 'shadow' for all-around, limitless personal growth, know that you're in good hands. With Jung's wisdom as our guiding star and an explorer's spirit, let's embark on this profound journey together.

1

NAVIGATING THE MIND'S MURKY WATERS WITH CARL JUNG

I magine Freud and Jung, two trailblazing explorers journeying through a forest, starting on the same path but soon finding themselves at a crossroads. While both were fervently mapping the vast expanse of the human psyche, their compass readings began to differ.

Freud perceived the unconscious as a thicket of personal traumas, desires, and suppressed memories. Like a dense, dark forest. In contrast, Jung envisioned an expansive national park. A place where individual woods were connected by a collective unconscious—a shared realm teeming with ancient symbols and narratives.

There's a legendary moment between these two pioneers. Amidst a fiery debate, the disagreement in the room grew so palpable that Freud, ever the stalwart, found himself so momentarily over-whelmed that he fainted! It wasn't just a sudden gust of wind; it was a storm of clashing visions.

GUIDING STARS OF JUNG'S EXPLORATION

Jung didn't just carve out a separate path. He introduced new navigation tools that would illuminate many an explorer's journey:

- Archetypes: Think of them as constellations in the night sky, universal patterns guiding our stories and actions—the Hero, the Sage, and more.
- Individuation: This is our personal quest, the individual journey each of us embarks on to discover, acknowledge, and integrate all facets of our psyche, especially those hidden trails.
- Collective Unconscious: Beyond our individual forests lies a grand interconnected landscape, filled with stories and symbols from ages past.
- The Shadow: Every explorer has one, especially when standing tall against the evening sun. This silhouette, formed from parts of ourselves we might not fully recognize, is essential to our self-understanding.

ECHOES THROUGH THE AGES

Jung's trailblazing discoveries weren't just confined to his era. His marks are visible on many of the paths we tread today:

- Modern Psychology: Therapists worldwide have adopted Jung's maps, assisting individuals in navigating their personal landscapes.
- Spiritual Heights: Felt an inexplicable connection during meditation or a spiritual retreat? You might've just had a rendezvous with the collective unconscious.
- Artistic and Literary Trails: From epics like "Star Wars" to literary masterpieces, Jung's influence on narratives is

undeniably profound, a testament to the universality of his discoveries.

So, intrepid traveler of the mind, as we gear up for our expedition, remember we're in good hands. With Jung's compass and wisdom by our side, we're set to embark on a quest of self-understanding and transformation. Let's embark.

The Role of the Shadow

Reflect on a recent situation where you witnessed a behavior or reaction in yourself that surprised you. Could this be an aspect of your 'shadow' emerging?

Conversing with Your Shadow

In a quiet space, have an imagined dialogue with your shadow. Write down the questions you'd like to ask it and pen down the responses that come instinctively to you. Example questions could include:

- *Why do you emerge in certain situations?*
- *What do you need from me?*
- *How can I better integrate you into my conscious self?*

Archetype Exploration

Jung believed in various archetypes like The Hero, The Mother, The Child, etc. Reflect on the various roles you play in your life and identify which Jungian archetypes resonate with you. For each, list out their positive traits and their shadow traits that you observe in yourself.

Integrating the Shadow

Can you think of a moment in literature, movies, or personal experiences where someone encountered and integrated their shadow? Describe the transformation you observed.

Jungian Vocabulary Builder

Create a list of terms you associate with Jungian psychology (e.g., archetype, collective unconscious). For each term, write a brief definition and illustrate it with a personal experience or observation.

The Collective Shadow

How do you think society's collective shadow manifests in today's world? Can you identify shared "shadows" within your community or globally?

Shadow Art

Using any art medium of your choice (drawing, painting, poetry, dance, etc.), express your understanding of the shadow concept. This doesn't need to be a masterpiece but a personal reflection of your engagement with Jung's idea.

2

DANCING WITH OUR SHADOW

In the expansive terrain of Jung's psychology, there lies a somewhat elusive yet profound concept: the Shadow. This chapter, akin to a gentle guide, will illuminate this shadowy domain, offering insights and clarity as we navigate its depth and significance in our own healing and personal growth.

THE SHADOW UNVEILED

At the core of Jung's psychology stands the "Shadow". While such a term might evoke images of a lingering silhouette or a dark twin, in Jung's perspective, it's far more nuanced. The Shadow is that unconscious segment of our personality holding our weaknesses, suppressed desires, and deep-seated instincts. Imagine a room in your mind's mansion that you seldom visit—it's dusty, dark, and holds items you've long forgotten or chosen to ignore.

EVERYDAY ENCOUNTERS WITH THE SHADOW

This may or may not come as a surprise, but the Shadow is remarkably present in our daily lives. Have you ever found yourself intensely disliking someone without a concrete reason? It's possible that the qualities you disdain in them are actually reflections of your own shadow, unseen and unrecognized aspects of yourself. Think of it as walking past a mirror without realizing it's reflecting a version of you you're not entirely familiar with.

JUNG'S PERSONAL ODYSSEY

There's nothing like a firsthand account to bring a concept to life. Jung wasn't just a theorist; he was his own experimental subject. During a period of deep self-exploration, Jung confronted his Shadow head-on. He described this as a "confrontation with the unconscious." This profound inner expedition paved the way to his masterwork, The Red Book. Within its pages, Jung chronicled his encounters with the various facets of his psyche, offering us not just a view into his mind but a blueprint for our own journeys.

SIGNIFICANCE IN PERSONAL GROWTH

Ironically, the Shadow might just be the beacon of light leading us to wholeness. Recognizing and integrating the Shadow is not about banishing the darkness but embracing it. It's a key step toward "individuation", a term Jung coined to describe the process of becoming the person one is inherently meant to be. Imagine piecing together a jigsaw puzzle; the shadowy pieces, though perhaps unsettling at first glance, are crucial in completing the picture. Embracing them leads to a more complete, balanced self—a healing process for past triggers and a release of blocked energies.

Journeying with Jung is never a mere academic exercise. It's an invitation, a beckoning hand towards understanding ourselves in ways we might never have anticipated.

LITERATURE & CINEMA'S DANCE WITH THE SHADOW

It's astounding how a concept, once confined to the corridors of analytical psychology, now dances in the limelight of novels, movies, and contemporary discourse. In the tapestry of literature, certain narratives seem to resonate with the essence of the Shadow. Take Robert Louis Stevenson's "Dr. Jekyll and Mr. Hyde" for instance. It's not merely a tale of a man and his alter ego; it's an intricate waltz with the Shadow. Jekyll's transformation into Hyde represents the embodiment of that part of us we sometimes fail to acknowledge. The darker urges lurking in the unconscious.

Switching from pages to the silver screen, the Shadow has had its moments of cinematic glory. In the dark alleys of "Fight Club", we witness the protagonist's tumultuous rendezvous with his shadow self. It's a visceral representation of the internal conflict many experience. "Black Swan" offers a ballet of duality, where the push and pull between the protagonist's inherent self and her darker desires showcase the raw power and allure of the Shadow.

THE SHADOW'S ECHO IN TODAY'S CONVERSATIONS

Beyond classics and celluloid, Jung's Shadow has found its voice in contemporary discussions too. Seminars, podcasts, and books often highlight the idea of confronting one's shadow, echoing Jung's belief in self-integration. Even in modern therapeutic techniques, the emphasis on recognizing and integrating the Shadow has become prevalent. It's as if the whole world is slowly warming up to the idea that embracing the darker facets of oneself is the pathway to holistic healing and growth.

Peeling back the layers of culture, one might be amazed at how deep Jung's influence runs. From the tales we tell to the discussions we engage in, the Shadow, with its depth and duality, is ever-present. As we continue our journey, it becomes evident: Jung's ideas aren't just theories on paper; they are living, breathing entities in our shared cultural psyche. As we delve deeper into the Shadow's realm, remember, it's a journey towards illumination. Ready to embrace and understand your own Shadow? Let's venture forth.

Diving into the Mind

Have you ever experienced a moment when something unexpected bubbled up from your unconscious mind? Perhaps it was a forgotten memory or a sudden emotion. Describe that experience.

Guiding questions on the next page

Triggering Moments: *Think back to the surroundings or circumstances when this unexpected thought or emotion surfaced. Was there a particular stimulus, like a song, scent, or even a casual remark, that might have triggered it?*

Initial Reaction: *How did you initially react when this memory or emotion emerged from your unconscious? Were you surprised, confused, overwhelmed, or perhaps even elated?*

Connecting the Dots: *As you reflect on that unexpected memory or emotion, can you identify any recent events or situations in your life that might be related or could have acted as a catalyst for this sudden emergence?*

Conscious Decisions

Reflect on a recent decision you made. How much of that decision do you believe was governed by your conscious mind, and how much was influenced by unconscious factors?

Guiding questions on the next page

Decision Details: *Describe the recent decision in detail. What was the situation? What options were you considering, and what did you ultimately decide?*

Rational Factors: *List down the logical reasons or conscious thought processes that contributed to your decision. Were there specific pros and cons you weighed? What objectives or outcomes were you aiming for with this choice?*

Gut Feelings & Undercurrents: *Reflect on any feelings, instincts, or intuitions you had during the decision-making process. Were there any unexplained inclinations or reservations you felt about a particular option? Could these feelings be hints from your unconscious mind?*

Two Minds Dialogue

Write a dialog between your conscious and unconscious mind. Start with a simple statement or decision, like "I want to buy that book." Let your conscious mind provide logical reasons, and then let your unconscious mind reveal deeper motivations or reservations.

The Ego's Play

Think about a time when you felt defensive or took something personally. In hindsight, do you believe it was your ego trying to protect your self-image?

Guiding questions on the next page

The Triggering Event: *Describe the specific event or situation that made you feel defensive or personally attacked. What was said or done, and how did you initially react?*

Ego's Defense: *Reflect on what aspect of your self-image felt threatened in that moment. Was it your competence, your kindness, your status, or perhaps another aspect of your identity?*

Reflection and Realization: *Now, with the benefit of hindsight, can you identify any patterns where your ego might have overreacted or played a more dominant role than necessary? How might you handle a similar situation differently in the future, knowing what you now understand about the ego's involvement?*

Ego Awareness

Spend a day actively monitoring your reactions and feelings, particularly during conflicts or challenges. Note down on your phone moments you feel your ego is influencing your responses. Reflect on alternative ways you could have reacted without the ego's interference.

Unconscious Influences

Can you identify any beliefs or behaviors you have that might stem from childhood or past experiences? How do these influence your current actions or decisions?

Guiding questions on the next page

Childhood Memories: *Reflect on a vivid memory from your childhood. Was there a phrase frequently spoken at home, or a particular incident that left an imprint? Describe that memory and how it made you feel.*

Current Behavior Link: *Can you see any parallels between how you felt during that childhood event and how you react in certain situations today? Is there a particular behavior, habit, or belief you now hold that might have roots in this memory?*

Decision-making Process: *Think of a recent decision you made. In retrospect, do you see any influence from your past experiences, especially from childhood, in this decision? How might recognizing these influences alter or affirm the choices you make moving forward?*

Deep Dive Visualization

Set aside 10 minutes for a meditative visualization. Imagine a vast ocean— the surface represents your conscious mind and the deep, dark depths represent your unconscious. Visualize diving into this ocean, going deeper and observing any symbols, memories, or feelings that arise. After your dive, journal about your observations.

The Role of Ego

How do you define your ego? Do you see it as a protector, a hindrance, a combination of both, or something else entirely?

Ego Reduction Practice

Choose a day to practice reducing your ego's influence. This might mean letting go of having the last word, not taking things personally, or stepping back from needing to be the center of attention. At the end of the day, reflect on the experience and how it felt to deliberately limit the role of your ego.

3

THE SHADOW'S GENTLE EMBRACE

As we've traversed the expanse of Jung's mind and ventured into the collective realm of culture, let's now bring the journey inward. Imagine holding a compass, its needle pointing directly to the heart of your being. Jung's Shadow Theory, when internalized, can serve as that compass, guiding you through the labyrinth of self-discovery in the modern age. Let's delve into the timeless wisdom embedded in this theory and moreover, translate it into actionable insights for you.

THE ROLE OF THE SHADOW IN PERSONAL DEVELOPMENT

Personal growth is akin to nurturing a garden. It involves tending, nurturing, and sometimes confronting those overgrown, shadowy corners. Embracing your Shadow is not about battling the overgrown weeds but understanding them at their root. By doing so, you illuminate areas of yourself that yearn for acknowledgment. The process paves the way for an authentic self-awareness, allowing you to evolve into the best version of yourself, free from the chains of suppressed emotions and hidden desires.

NAVIGATING DAILY LIFE WITH THE WISDOM OF THE SHADOW

Think of the last time you reacted strongly to someone's words or actions. Was it truly about them, or was it a dance with your Shadow? Recognizing this dynamic can transform our interpersonal relationships. By understanding our Shadow, we reduce those knee-jerk reactions, making way for compassion and deeper connections. It's like adjusting the focus on a camera; things become clearer, relationships become richer, and life, more harmonious.

As we navigate this enlightening path, let's pause and reflect upon the words of Carl Jung: "Everyone carries a shadow, and the less it is embodied in the individual's conscious life, the blacker and denser it is." Read that again, then take a moment to let these words resonate. Your journey towards integrating your shadow is not just about dispelling the darkness but recognizing the light that emerges from understanding it. The shadow isn't a flaw; it's a facet, and by acknowledging it, you're on your way to a richer, fuller life.

In the bustling realms of modern life, where distractions are many and moments of reflection are few, the lessons of the Shadow offer clarity and guidance. It's a gentle reminder that beneath the layers of roles we play and masks we wear, lies a truth waiting to be acknowledged. Journey on, with the Shadow as your gentle guide, towards a world of inner peace and authentic living.

Shadow Acknowledgment

Before you can work with your shadow, you must first recognize it.

Reflect: Can you recall a recent moment when you overreacted or felt an intense emotion out of proportion to the situation? Describe the event and your reaction.

The Shadow Journal

Set aside a special journal just for shadow work. Every night for a week, write down situations where you felt uncomfortable emotions, or times when you think your shadow self might have influenced your behavior.

Uncovering the Why

Shadow work isn't just about identifying the shadow but understanding its origins.

Think about a trait or behavior you don't like in others. Do you ever exhibit this behavior yourself, even if in a subtle way? Why do you think this particular trait triggers such a reaction in you?

Dialogue with the Shadow

Engage in a written dialogue with your shadow. Start by writing a question or a statement addressing your shadow. Then, let your hand freely write whatever comes to mind in response, as if your shadow is answering. This can provide direct insights into hidden parts of your psyche.

The Light and Dark Balance

Shadow work is not about eliminating the shadow but understanding and integrating it.

Reflect: Can you identify a situation where what you once considered a negative trait actually benefited you? For instance, perhaps your stubbornness allowed you to stand firm in a crucial situation.

SECTION 2

THE PSYCHE: THE EVER-EXPANDING MANSION OF THE SELF

When you hear the term "psyche", what comes to mind? For many, it might evoke thoughts of the brain, the mind, or perhaps even the soul. But for Jung, the psyche was a grand, all-encompassing term, a realm vast and intricate. Imagine standing before a sprawling mansion, each door promising a story, each room holding secrets. That's the psyche for you.

Jung's definition of the psyche is reminiscent of the vastness and mystery of the cosmos. He didn't limit it merely to thoughts and feelings of which we're aware. Instead, he plunged deeper, pulling into its fold the vast ocean of unconscious thoughts, memories, desires, and archetypes that lie dormant.

As you stand in the foyer of this mansion, the rooms bathed in sunlight represent the conscious mind. It's familiar and comforting because these rooms are the parts of ourselves we recognize. But then, there are rooms draped in shadows, perhaps even locked, which represent the unconscious. These hold memories we've forgotten, feelings we've suppressed, and the universal archetypes we all share. Can you feel the tug, the gentle whisper urging you to explore?

JUNG'S DREAM HOUSE: AN ILLUMINATING JOURNEY

Let me take you on a little detour. In his works, Jung narrated a recurring dream. He dreamt of a grand, multi-storied house. The ground floor was traditionally furnished, representing the conscious, the present. As he explored further, venturing upstairs, the house became older, perhaps pointing to the first layer of the unconscious filled with personal memories.

But the most profound moment came when he descended to the basement. Here, he found himself in a beautifully preserved Roman cellar, hinting at ancient, collective memories shared across genera-

SHADOW WORK DEEP DIVE JOURNAL | 49

tions. Further down, he discovered caves filled with primitive tools, taking him back to the dawn of humanity.

Isn't that an evocative representation of the psyche? Just as in his dream house, our psyche isn't just about the present moment or personal past. It's a tapestry woven with threads from the dawn of human existence.

Dear reader, understanding the psyche, this expansive mansion, is the first step to unlocking the rooms within, especially the shadowy corners we're often hesitant to explore. But remember, it's in the dimly lit spaces that the most profound discoveries about ourselves often lie. Ready to take a step closer?

———————

4

THE PSYCHE: A THEATER OF SELF-DISCOVERY

When you think about yourself, do you ever imagine you're part of a grand performance? A theater where you're both the actor and the audience, the director and the stagehand? Our psyche is remarkably like that, a theater with layers, intricacies, and an ancient foundation. Let's part the curtains.

THE CONSCIOUS MIND: THE ONGOING PLAY

Every day, as you go about your life, you're actively participating in a play. Every thought you consciously process, every memory you recall at will, every emotion you feel and recognize – all of this happens on the stage of your conscious mind. The conversations you have, the decisions you make. And all those times you laugh, cry, ponder, or daydream, they're scenes from the current play of your life. But what's happening off-stage?

PERSONAL UNCONSCIOUS: THE BACKSTAGE MYSTIQUE

Hidden just behind the curtain lies a fascinating realm. It's the backstage, cluttered with props from past performances, scripts from shows you thought you had forgotten, and emotions you tucked away, thinking they were too painful or embarrassing to confront. The personal unconscious is the custodian of your personal history. Some vividly remembered, and some dimly lit.

Let me tell you about Linda. Linda had a recurring dream that always left her puzzled. In it, she'd see a faceless man in a park. Each time the dream recurred, she felt a strange mix of fear and familiarity. Seeking answers, Linda went through therapy. There, she unraveled a forgotten memory: as a child, she had once been lost in a park and was comforted by a kind stranger till her parents found her. This suppressed memory, a performance from her past, was trying to resurface, reminding Linda of her vulnerabilities and the kindness of strangers.

COLLECTIVE UNCONSCIOUS: THE ANCIENT THEATER

Deeper than the backstage, beneath the very structure of the theater, lies the bedrock, the collective unconscious. It's not about 'you' or 'me'. It's about 'us', as a species. Here, you find universal scripts, age-old archetypes like The Hero, The Mother, The Wise Old Man. These are tales, emotions, symbols, and motifs humanity has shared across time. Unbeknownst to our conscious minds, but influencing the plays we put on, nevertheless.

TALES AS OLD AS TIME

Isn't it fascinating that cultures separated by vast oceans and millennia have spun tales with uncannily similar themes? Why does almost every culture have a story of a great flood, or a tale of star-crossed lovers? Could it be that these stories, though dressed in local garments, spring from the same ancient foundation? It's the collective unconscious at play, showcasing shared human experiences.

You see, understanding our psyche's theater is essential. Not just to appreciate the play we're currently a part of, but to recognize the influences, memories, and ancient tales that shape our performances. It's a journey of introspection, of unearthing, and above all, of understanding the grand narrative that is 'you'.

Exploring the Backstage

Set aside some quiet time to dig into your "personal unconscious," the backstage area where props and scripts from your past are stored.

Take a journal and jot down any recurring dreams or emotions that you've pushed to the back of your mind.

Can you identify any 'props' or 'scripts' from your past that might be influencing your current 'performance'?

Reflect on these findings; what can you integrate into your current life from your past experiences?

Recurring Dreams

Much like Linda's recurring dream, do you have any recurring dreams or thoughts that puzzle you?

Describe the recurring dream or thought.

What emotions does it evoke?

Have you tried to dig deeper to understand its origins? If yes, what have you discovered?

Tales as Old as Time

Reflect on a myth, fairy tale, or cultural story that you feel deeply connected to.

What is the story?

Why do you feel connected to it?

Could this connection be an influence from the collective unconscious, a shared human experience? Why or why not?

Deleted Scenes

In every production, some scenes are cut and never see the light of day. Think about decisions or actions you almost took but eventually didn't.

Describe a moment you 'cut' from your life's 'script.'

What led you to cut this scene?

Do you ever wonder what would have happened if that 'scene' had been included in your life?

5

ARCHETYPES: THE RECURRING ROLES IN OUR THEATER

Have you ever noticed that some stories, regardless of where they originate, feel eerily familiar? Or have you found that certain characters in tales from opposite ends of the world bear a striking resemblance to one another? Like how every culture seems to have its own version of a hero, a wise sage, or even a mischief-maker. These aren't mere coincidences. They're what Carl Jung would call 'archetypes', and they form an essential part of our psychological theater. Let's dive in, shall we?

ARCHETYPES: THE UNIVERSAL SYMBOLS WE CAN'T ESCAPE

Archetypes, in Jung's framework, are like the classic roles in our theater. They're universal symbols, patterns, or characters that show up time and again. And not just in tales or myths, but also in our dreams, behaviors, and even aspirations. They resonate with us not because they're personal; they're universal. They tap into our collective unconscious, the foundational bedrock we explored in the last chapter. This is where their power and significance lie – they connect us to shared human experiences, creating a bond that stretches across cultures and ages.

Let's introduce you to some of the main players:

- The Hero: Often found embarking on quests, overcoming gargantuan challenges, and returning transformed. Think of King Arthur, Mulan, or even Harry Potter.
- The Mother: The nurturing, protective figure. She could be the loving embrace you come home to, or the fierce protector warding off any threat. From Mother Earth myths to characters like Molly Weasley in modern tales, she's omnipresent.
- The Wise Old Man: This is the guru, the mentor. He offers guidance, often propelling the hero forward in their journey. Think Gandalf from The Lord of the Rings or Mr. Miyagi from The Karate Kid.
- The Trickster: Ah, the mischief-maker! They challenge the status quo, sometimes creating chaos, but often leading to profound change and growth. Loki from Norse mythology or even Jack Sparrow could fit this bill.

A FASCINATING GLIMPSE FROM JUNG'S NOTEBOOK

Let me share an enchanting tale from Jung's own experience. Jung once noticed an intriguing pattern with two of his patients. These two were from wildly different cultural backgrounds – one from the heart of Europe and another from a remote part of Asia. Yet they presented dreams with strikingly similar elements. Both dreamt of a wise old serpent, a symbol neither had encountered in their personal lives. Jung was convinced: This wasn't mere coincidence. It was the Wise Old Man archetype, manifesting as a serpent, making its presence felt, revealing the universal threads that bind us in the grand tapestry of human experience.

Every time you read a story, watch a movie, or even recall a dream, try spotting these archetypes. Recognize them, and you'll feel a connection, not just to the narrative but to the countless generations before you who have been captivated by the same patterns. You see, understanding archetypes isn't just academic; it's deeply personal. It reminds us that in our individual stories, we are not alone; we are part of something larger, timeless, and deeply interconnected. How's that for a profound encore?

Identifying Archetypes in Your Life

The collective unconscious hosts universal scripts and roles that we all share.

Identify an archetype (e.g., The Hero, The Mother) that resonates with you.

Why do you think this archetype is significant in your life?

Can you pinpoint experiences or beliefs that might have shaped this archetype's importance to you?

The Script of Your Conscious Mind

Think about your day-to-day life as a performance on a stage. What roles do you often find yourself playing? Are you the hero, the sidekick, or perhaps the villain in some scenarios?

List three roles you commonly play in your daily life.

Describe a recent scenario for each role.

How do you feel about these roles? Would you like to change them?

The Ensemble Cast

No one acts alone; we all have an ensemble cast of characters who play roles in our life's story.

Who are the supporting characters in your life's play?

What roles do they play? Are they mentors, antagonists, comic relief?

How do these characters enrich or complicate your journey?

6

THE PSYCHE'S PATH TO WHOLENESS

Ever felt like you're constantly at war with yourself? One part of you craves adventure while another craves the comfort of home. One part seeks the limelight, while another shies away. The psyche is a complex realm, and harmonizing its intricate parts is no simple task. But, it's precisely this harmonization that leads us to a fulfilling, whole life.

INDIVIDUATION: YOUR PERSONAL SYMPHONY

Imagine an orchestra. Each instrument has its distinct sound. Sometimes, when not tuned or played well, can seem out of sync with the rest. Individuation is the art of orchestrating these diverse sounds, these parts of our psyche, into a harmonious symphony. It's not about discarding or disliking certain instruments but understanding and integrating each one's unique tune. Through individuation, we aim to reconcile and embrace all aspects of our being, from our conscious thoughts to our deepest unconscious desires.

THE DANCE OF DUALITY

Now, the trick is in understanding that our psyche thrives on duality. We have:

- Light and Dark: Instead of fearing the shadow, recognize its purpose. It's the contrast that makes the light meaningful.
- Masculine and Feminine: Irrespective of gender, we all have masculine (assertive, logical) and feminine (intuitive, nurturing) energies. Embracing both creates harmony.
- Conscious and Unconscious: Our conscious mind is just the tip of the iceberg. By diving deep and acknowledging the vast unconscious, we enrich our life experience.

Achieving balance doesn't always, or even usually mean a 50-50 split. It's about respecting and understanding both sides, allowing them to coexist, dance, and sometimes even spar, but always aiming for a dynamic equilibrium.

FROM CRISIS TO CLARITY: A TALE OF TRANSFORMATION

Let me share with you a story that might feel close to home for many. Alex, a driven corporate lawyer in his late 40s, experienced what many would call a midlife crisis. Feeling a deep void, despite his accolades, he took a sabbatical and traveled. On the serene beaches of Bali, amidst the mountains of the Andes, and in the bustling markets of Marrakech, he met parts of himself he never knew existed.

He laughed. He cried. He danced. He meditated.

Alex realized his logical, assertive side, which served him so well in the courtroom, was only half the story. He discovered a nurturing, intuitive side, which found joy in silence, in art, in just being. By journey's end, Alex returned not just with souvenirs but with a soul more in tune with its various melodies.

Understanding the psyche isn't an intellectual exercise; it's a deeply personal journey. And while the path might be strewn with challenges, the destination is profound peace and joy. As you move forward, remember that every aspect of you has its role in this grand theater. By recognizing and loving each part, you're not only healing past triggers and wounds but also setting the stage for a life of deeper connections, understanding, and bliss. So, take a bow, and let your personal symphony play on.

Your Personal Symphony

Reflect on your own process of individuation. What "instruments" in your personal symphony do you feel are out of tune? How can you integrate them to create a harmonious melody?

Identify any "instruments" (aspects of yourself) that feel out of tune.

What steps can you take to better integrate this part into your life?

How would achieving this integration affect your sense of inner peace and fulfillment?

Exploring Duality

Allocate some quiet time to journal about the dualities within your own personality. Examine your masculine and feminine sides, your light and dark, your conscious and unconscious self.

Describe an occasion where your masculine traits took the lead.

Recount a moment where your feminine side was more prominent.

Reflect on an instance where your shadow self came into the light.

Identifying Your Shadows

Make a list of traits you admire in others and traits you don't like. Now, reflect on whether these traits are shadows within yourself that you haven't recognized yet.

What traits in others do you admire?

What traits in others irritate you?

How do these traits manifest in your own behavior, whether overtly or subtly?

Soul Searching

Imagine taking a sabbatical like Alex did. If you had the opportunity to discover untapped parts of yourself, where would you go and what would you do?

Describe your dream destination for soul-searching.

What activities or experiences would you pursue?

What parts of yourself do you think you might discover or get to know better?

SECTION 3

HOW TO DO SHADOW WORK

Ah, dear reader, we've journeyed through the depths of understanding the shadow and the intricate theater of our psyche. But now, we approach a crossroads—how do you actively engage with that ever-elusive shadow?

Many might ask, "Why embark on such a journey?" Well, let's start by painting a picture: Imagine being on a boat, smoothly sailing through the waters, only to find yourself continuously being pulled off course by an invisible anchor. That anchor is, in many ways, akin to our shadow—a hidden force, subtly dictating our life's path. Usually in ways we aren't even aware of.

Shadow work is about diving deep, discovering that anchor, understanding its weight, and deciding how we want to navigate with or without it. And just like any profound journey, the destination—though significant—pales in comparison to the revelations and transformations the journey itself brings forth.

You might be wondering, is it worth the potential emotional storms? Well, here's the liberating truth: Confronting the shadow is a direct confrontation with oneself. Yes, it's challenging, like scaling a mountain where each altitude presents its own set of trials. But oh, the view from the top and the elation in every breath of air—it's unmatched.

Think about this: How many times have you felt trapped by repeating patterns? Ever wondered why certain triggers push your buttons while others don't? Or why particular emotions flood you, seemingly out of the blue? These are not random misfires of your being but rather clues, guiding lights pointing towards areas yearning for your attention and understanding.

This section, dear traveler, is dedicated to arming you with the tools and encouragement needed as you embark on this transformative journey. For in understanding and integrating the shadow, you're not just finding pieces of yourself; you're crafting a more harmonious, balanced, and authentic life narrative.

Jung once remarked, "Until you make the unconscious conscious, it will direct your life, and you will call it fate." Shadow work, at its core, is about shining a light into those dim, often overlooked corners of our psyche. While the journey might seem daunting, multiple paths lead toward understanding.

Here are the 4 techniques we'll be exploring, with many shadow prompts and questions to use as guide rails:

- Dream Analysis
- Active Imagination
- Guided Meditations and Visualizations
- Journaling

So, are you ready? The path is challenging, but the rewards are life-changing. Let's embark on this journey of shadow work together, unlocking doors to your deepest self, and lighting up corridors you never knew existed within your soul.

7

PREPARING FOR SHADOW WORK

The path to self-discovery isn't always paved with daisies and sunshine. Sometimes, it requires a flashlight and the courage to explore where sunlight doesn't reach. Shadow work, in essence, is that exploration—venturing into the darkness to discover what's been hidden, denied, or suppressed within us. Much like a ship navigating treacherous waters requires a skilled captain, a sturdy vessel, and a reliable compass, so does this inner exploration need its own set of tools and strategies. This chapter, dear reader, is your guide to set sail into the deep, vast ocean of your inner world. Let's start by reminding you of the need for shadow work.

WHY ENGAGE IN SHADOW WORK?

Imagine a life where your reactions are not just knee-jerk responses to old wounds. A life where relationships blossom not out of mutual trauma, but out of mutual understanding and authenticity. Sounds dreamy, doesn't it? Well, that's the magic of shadow work including but not limited to:

- Emotional Healing: Ever felt an emotion so strong it took you by surprise? Shadow work can help you trace back these emotions, understand them, and heal from the roots.
- Better Relationships: By understanding our own triggers and suppressed emotions, we can navigate relationships with more empathy and less projection. We interact as our true selves, not as wounded versions reacting to past traumas.
- Understanding Self-sabotaging Behaviors: Those moments when you've been on the brink of success and then, inexplicably, you pull back? Shadow work can uncover the deep-seated fears and beliefs that hold you back.
- Fostering Personal Growth: True growth occurs when we're not just dealing with the surface but are courageously diving deep, challenging our inner narratives, and rewriting our stories in a way that aligns with our authentic self.

THE SIGNS THAT SHADOW WORK IS NEEDED

There's a misconception that only those who have experienced trauma need this kind of introspective work. The truth is that we all have areas of our psyche that need light. Some signs that hint at a lurking shadow include:

- Persistent Patterns of Problems in Relationships: If you find that your relationships—be it romantic, familial, or friendly —follow the same tumultuous pattern, it might be time to look within. This includes the Cycle of Toxic Relationships.
- Recurring Negative Emotions Without Clear Triggers: Do certain situations or people spark a strong, often negative, emotion out of proportion to the event? This can be a sign of a deeper issue at play.
- Unexplainable Fears or Phobias: If you've ever had an irrational fear or a phobia and thought, "Where did this

come from?" it might be a shadow screaming for your attention.

Let me share a story about Clara. Clara had a perplexing pattern: she constantly found herself drawn to partners who were emotionally unavailable. Each relationship, no matter how different, echoed the same sentiments of neglect and emotional distance. She decided to explore this pattern through shadow work with the help of a therapist.

The journey was tough. Naturally. As they delved deeper, a forgotten memory surfaced—a young Clara, all of seven, left at a boarding school by her parents. The feeling of abandonment, the nights crying into her pillow, and the yearning to be seen and comforted had cast a long shadow on her adult life. By recognizing this shadow, Clara could see the link between her childhood experience and her adult relationship choices. It was her psyche's way of trying to rewrite the past, to find someone distant and make them stay.

With this revelation, Clara's journey of healing began. No longer did she seek relationships to mend her past. Instead, she sought them to enrich her present.

Dear reader, as you contemplate your own journey, remember Clara's story. Sometimes, what seems like an unrelated pattern has deep roots in the past. By shining a light on these shadows, by understanding them, we don't just heal; we free ourselves to craft a future based on choice, not unconscious patterns.

CREATING A SAFE SPACE

Before you dive in, you need to set up a safe base—a sanctuary where you can be vulnerable, open, and introspective without inhibition.

Physical Environment: Choose a place where you feel comfortable —be it a quiet corner of your home, a peaceful garden, or a serene beach. It should be a spot where distractions are minimal, where you can truly be with yourself.

Mental Environment: This is equally if not more crucial. You're preparing to face parts of yourself that you might have ignored or suppressed. It's vital to approach this with an open heart and a non-judgmental mindset. Imagine you're meeting a younger version of yourself—how would you treat them? With harsh words or gentle understanding? Cultivate the latter.

TOOLS OF THE TRADE

Over the centuries, explorers have used various tools to navigate their journeys. For our inner voyage, these tools might look a bit different, but they're just as essential.

Journals: Writing can be therapeutic. It not only captures your thoughts but also allows you to reflect on them. A journal specifically for shadow work can become your confidante, capturing your insights, fears, and growth.

Meditation Aids: Guided meditations or visualization exercises can be powerful allies. They help calm the mind, making it more receptive to introspection.

Therapeutic Aids: There are numerous cards, books, and interactive tools designed specifically for shadow work. They can provide structure and direction to your exploration.

The Importance of Patience

Patience is key. If there's one thing to keep in mind, it's this. Shadow work isn't a weekend retreat; it's a pilgrimage. There will be moments of clarity, but there will also be days of confusion.

Remember, growth, like nature, has its own rhythm.

THE SKEPTIC'S TRANSFORMATION

Meet Alex. A pragmatist to the core, he initially approached shadow work with a hefty dose of skepticism. "How could journaling and some meditation help me understand myself better?" he mused. Nevertheless, a lingering sense of restlessness prompted him to try.

The initial days were challenging. Frustrated by the lack of 'instant results,' Alex was on the brink of giving up. But he persisted…with a little encouragement. Months turned into years, and what began as a skeptical experiment transformed into a soulful journey. By treading slowly and steadily, Alex unearthed long-buried emotions, healing wounds he didn't even know existed.

To this day, Alex maintains that it was his commitment to the process, not the desire for a quick outcome, that truly made the difference. It's about focusing on the inputs first, not the outputs.

So, are you ready to embark on this transformative voyage? Remember, it's not about how fast you travel, but about the insights, understanding, and healing you gather along the way. Equip yourself, prepare your vessel, and set sail with patience and hope. The treasures you'll discover within are well worth the journey.

8

DREAM ANALYSIS: UNLOCKING THE NIGHT'S MYSTERIES

I magine if your mind wrote a nightly letter to you, filled with insights, warnings, and lessons. Dreams, you see, are those letters penned in the unique ink of symbols and emotions. Dream analysis is akin to decoding these cryptic notes, revealing clues about our inner world, wounds, desires, and much more.

WHAT IS DREAM ANALYSIS?

At its core, dream analysis is the art and science of interpreting our dreams. Rooted in the works of Freud and Jung, it recognizes that every dream carries significant meaning. Contrary to often popular belief, they are far from being just random narratives. Dreams offer us a window into our unconscious mind. They speak in a symbolic language, revealing to us the issues that we may not be consciously aware of during our waking hours.

THE BIRTH OF PSYCHOANALYSIS

Sigmund Freud, an Austrian neurologist, stands as one of the most influential figures in the world of psychology. Born in 1856, Freud pioneered the development of psychoanalysis, a method of treatment and a theory of the mind. It proposed that unconscious desires, memories, and conflicts significantly impact behavior and emotions. Freud's ground-breaking ideas were controversial during his time, challenging both scientific and social norms. But they've certainly stood the test of time.

His initial work with patients, particularly those with hysteria, led him to uncover the deep-seated traumas that seemed to manifest as physical symptoms. Through extensive conversations, or "talk therapy," he unearthed the power of the unconscious mind.

THE ROLE OF DREAMS IN THE PSYCHOANALYTIC MODEL

For Freud, dreams held a particular fascination. He viewed them as the "royal road to the unconscious," offering a glimpse into the hidden recesses of the mind. In his seminal work, "The Interpretation of Dreams" (1900), Freud proposed that dreams are not mere random occurrences but are deeply connected to our wishes, fears, and unresolved conflicts.

Dreams, according to the psychoanalytic model, serve as safety valves, allowing the psyche to address and process suppressed desires without the constraints of societal judgment or consciousness. They became a crucial tool in psychoanalytic therapy, revealing insights into a patient's inner world. Personally I find this fascinating, and I hope you do too.

THE STRUCTURE OF DREAMS

Freud suggested that every dream has two primary components:

Manifest Content: This is the dream as we remember it upon waking. It's the storyline, characters, images, and emotions that populate the dream. Often, the manifest content can be bewildering, nonsensical, or seemingly irrelevant.

Latent Content: Hidden beneath the surface narrative of the dream lies its true meaning or the latent content. This content represents the unconscious wishes, desires, and conflicts that are too threatening or taboo for the dreamer's conscious mind to handle directly.

The process of dream analysis involves decoding the manifest content to uncover the latent content, revealing the dream's true significance.

THE PROCESS OF DREAM-WORK: CONDENSATION, DISPLACEMENT, SYMBOLIZATION, AND SECONDARY ELABORATION

Dream-work refers to the mechanisms the mind uses to transform the latent dream thoughts into the actual dream (manifest content). Freud identified several key processes:

- Condensation: Multiple ideas, individuals, and concepts from the dreamer's life might merge into a single symbol or scene in a dream. This compression means each dream element can have multiple meanings.
- Displacement: This involves shifting emotional intensity from one idea or object to another, less threatening one. For example, feelings about a boss might be displaced onto a dream about a schoolteacher.

- Symbolization: The mind often represents taboo desires or fears through symbols. A simple object in a dream can stand for something entirely different in the dreamer's waking life.
- Secondary Elaboration: Upon waking, the conscious mind tries to make sense of the dream. This process involves adding logical structure or coherence to the dream, even if the original dream lacked such logic.

Through these processes, the mind crafts dreams, both hiding and revealing our deepest desires and fears. By understanding and studying these processes, Freud believed one could decipher the hidden messages within our nocturnal narratives.

HOW UNFULFILLED WISHES FROM WAKING LIFE MANIFEST IN DREAMS

Freud posited that at the heart of every dream lies a wish. These wishes often arise from our daily lives, but because they remain unfulfilled, the mind seeks resolution in sleep. For instance, someone who is denied affection during waking hours might dream of a loving embrace. Such dreams provide a form of psychological relief, allowing for the expression of wishes that, for various reasons, aren't realized in reality.

THE SIGNIFICANCE OF CHILDHOOD EXPERIENCES AND DESIRES

Freud believed that our earliest experiences have a deep, lasting impact on our psyche. Dreams, in his view, often harken back to these formative years. For example, dreams of being chased might relate to childhood feelings of vulnerability, while dreams of flying could reflect early desires for freedom and autonomy. These dreams underscore the unresolved tensions or unmet desires from childhood that continue to influence the adult subconscious mind.

COMMON CRITICISMS OF FREUD'S DREAM THEORY

As groundbreaking as Freud's theories were, they weren't without detractors. Here are some common criticisms:

- **Overemphasis on Sexual Symbols:** Many believe Freud overly sexualized dream symbols. Not every dream symbol, critics argue, can be traced back to a repressed sexual desire.
- **Subjectivity:** Freud's method of interpretation was considered by some to be overly subjective, allowing for multiple, sometimes conflicting, interpretations of the same dream.
- **Limited Scope:** Some psychologists argue that Freud's emphasis on repressed desires neglects other significant aspects of the human experience in dreams, such as problem-solving or memory consolidation.
- **Not Universally Applicable:** Critics argue that his interpretations might not universally apply to individuals from different cultures or time periods. For example, what might be a taboo or repressed desire in Freud's Vienna might be commonplace and accepted in another culture or era.

THE FREUD FEUD

Remember Carl Jung? Well, as we touched on before, he was initially a close collaborator and friend of Sigmund Freud. Both shared an interest in the unconscious mind, but their paths diverged due to fundamental disagreements in their theories. While Freud's emphasis was on the personal experiences of the individual, particularly childhood and repressed desires, Jung sought to explore deeper, more universal aspects of the psyche.

Jung respected Freud's contributions but believed the scope of psychoanalysis was too narrow. He felt that there were elements of the unconscious that were collective and not solely shaped by personal experiences. This divergence in thought eventually led to a personal and professional split between the two giants of early psychoanalysis (not to forget the dramatic faint).

THE CONCEPT OF INDIVIDUATION: THE LIFELONG JOURNEY OF SELF-REALIZATION

A cornerstone of Jung's psychological theory is the process of individuation. This process refers to the individual's journey to become the person they are inherently meant to be. It's a voyage of self-realization, where one integrates different aspects of the unconscious into conscious awareness.

Individuation involves confronting and assimilating the 'shadow' (the darker, unknown parts of oneself), acknowledging and balancing masculine and feminine energies (Animus and Anima), and ultimately realizing the 'Self'—a harmonious unification of all components of the psyche. Dreams, even for Jung, play a crucial role in this journey, offering symbolic guidance and insights to the dreamer.

THE COLLECTIVE UNCONSCIOUS

The collective unconscious is one of Jung's most influential and controversial concepts. Unlike the personal unconscious, which is a repository of an individual's feelings, memories, and thoughts that are not currently conscious, the collective unconscious houses memories and ideas that are shared by all of humanity.

Jung proposed that this shared reservoir contains experiences and memories from our ancestral past—universal themes, stories, and motifs that have been passed down through generations. While the personal unconscious is shaped by individual experiences, the collective unconscious is the same for all humans, irrespective of culture or history.

HOW DREAMS HELP INTEGRATE SHADOW ASPECTS AND CONFRONT INNER TRUTHS

The process of individuation requires confronting and integrating one's 'shadow', which represents the lesser-known or suppressed parts of oneself. Dreams, in Jung's view, play a pivotal role in this. In the dream world, individuals often come face-to-face with characters or situations that reflect their shadow, forcing them to acknowledge and engage with these hidden aspects. Whether through confronting dream adversaries or navigating challenging scenarios, individuals are symbolically processing and integrating these shadow elements.

ANALYZING DREAM SYMBOLS: PERSONAL VS. UNIVERSAL

For Jung, dream symbols could have both personal and universal significance. A snake, for instance, might be a personal fear for someone who had a traumatic experience with one. But universally, snakes also symbolize transformation due to their shedding skin, and in some cultures, they are seen as symbols of wisdom or danger.

This dual nature means dream interpretation in the Jungian sense requires discerning between personal memories or traumas and the broader archetypal significance of symbols. The context of the dreamer's life, as well as the universal meanings of symbols, should both be considered.

ANIMA, ANIMUS, AND THE SELF IN DREAMS

The Anima and Animus, in Jungian psychology, represent the feminine side of a man and the masculine side of a woman, respectively. Dreams can often portray these aspects, providing insights into how one relates to these energies. A man dreaming of a powerful female figure might be coming to terms with his Anima or feminine side.

If these aspects appear distorted or confrontational in dreams, it might indicate an imbalance or unresolved tension related to these energies.

Dreams also frequently touch on the idea of 'The Self', which for Jung represented the unification of the conscious and unconscious, the culmination of individuation. Dreams that hint at this harmonious integration—like melding of opposites or reconciling with adversaries—suggest progress towards achieving wholeness. Analyzing these dreams can aid individuals in understanding where they are in their journey and what steps they might need to take towards self-realization.

CRITICISMS AND INTERPRETATIONS

The idea of a collective unconscious and archetypes, while influential, has faced criticism for its lack of empirical evidence. It's challenging to scientifically validate the existence of a shared psychic structure across humanity. Critics argue that while certain symbols may appear across cultures, it could be due to shared human experiences rather than a collective psychic structure.

While many of Jung's ideas aren't at the forefront of mainstream psychological practice today, they've left an indelible mark on overall psychology and the world. Some modern therapists use Jungian dream analysis as a tool to help patients explore their inner worlds, though often in conjunction with other therapeutic techniques.

Moreover, Jung's influence can be seen in broader cultural studies. His ideas on archetypes have been applied to literature, film, and art analysis, offering insights into the universal themes that resonate with humanity across time and space.

HOW DREAMS COMMUNICATE WITH THE SUBCONSCIOUS

Dreams as Expressions of Suppressed Emotions or Desires

At the heart of many psychotherapeutic modalities lies the belief that dreams serve as windows to our deeper selves. In sleep, the ego's defenses are lowered, and the subconscious emerges in the form of dreams. When trying to heal or integrate suppressed aspects of themselves, understanding dreams can be invaluable.

Often, suppressed emotions—those too overwhelming, embarrassing, or painful to acknowledge in waking life—find their voice in dreams. These emotions could stem from past traumas, societal conditioning, or personal fears. A person who has suppressed their feelings of anger might dream of an uncontrollable fire, while someone denying feelings of confinement might dream of being trapped.

Unresolved conflicts, whether internal or external, are frequent dream themes. These could range from interpersonal issues to inner battles between one's desires and moral compass. Dreams can offer a symbolic battleground, providing scenarios where these conflicts play out.

For instance, someone struggling to accept a part of their identity might dream of shadows or doppelgangers. Similarly, feelings of guilt or regret might manifest as being pursued or judged in a dream.

DREAM THERAPY IN PSYCHOLOGICAL HEALING

Dream therapy aims to interpret dreams to use them as tools for healing. In this therapeutic approach, the therapist and client work together to delve into the dream's symbolism, exploring its links to the dreamer's waking life, past traumas, and suppressed feelings.

In the context of shadow work, if you haven't guessed by now, dreams can be particularly telling. They might encounter dream characters or situations that represent parts of themselves they've rejected or neglected. By confronting and engaging with these dream elements, they can begin the process of acceptance and integration in their waking life.

ADDRESSING TRAUMA AND PHOBIAS THROUGH DREAM WORK

Traumatic events often leave an indelible mark on the psyche, and they frequently re-emerge in dreams. Someone who has experienced a traumatic event might relive it in their dreams or encounter symbolic representations of the trauma.

In dream therapy, these recurring trauma-related dreams can be approached with care and compassion, helping the individual process the trauma rather than be continually re-traumatized by it. Techniques such as dream re-scripting, where the dreamer reimagines the dream with a positive or empowering outcome, can be particularly effective.

Similarly, phobias or deep-seated fears might also play out in dreams. By addressing these fears in the dream context, it's possible to reduce their intensity and influence in the waking world.

While on a healing journey, understanding and integrating dream content can be transformative. Dreams provide a non-judgmental space to face one's fears, regrets, and suppressed emotions, offering a path to healing and wholeness. Now it's time to practically explore how you can apply this information to yourself for your own healing.

DREAM JOURNALS: THE WHY AND HOW

It all starts with the 'why'. Dream journals are foundational tools for anyone serious about understanding their dreams. The act of recording dreams not only aids in retaining dream details but also signals to the subconscious mind that dreams are valuable and worth remembering.

So it helps with:

- **Emotional Insights:** Unpack suppressed emotions or unresolved traumas.
- **Understanding Repetitive Behaviors:** Decipher patterns that might be sabotaging your personal or professional life.
- **Guidance and Intuition:** Your unconscious might be nudging you toward a decision or away from potential pitfalls.

Who's Best Suited for Dream Analysis?

Frankly, anyone can benefit. But if you're someone who:

- Often remembers dreams.
- Feels stuck in life and is looking for answers.
- Is intrigued by the realm of the unconscious and wants to explore deeper layers of the self.

Then dream analysis could be a valuable tool for you.

Which brings us to the 'how'. When you wake, before any other activity, jot down everything you can remember from your dreams. Even if it seems fragmented or nonsensical, write it down. Over time, you may begin to see patterns, recurring symbols, or narratives that offer insights into your shadow self or unresolved traumas.

THE SIGNIFICANCE OF SYMBOLS, MOTIFS, AND THEMES

Dreams often communicate through symbols—images or scenarios that carry specific meanings or emotions. Recognizing recurring symbols, motifs, or overarching themes in your dreams can provide clues to suppressed emotions, unresolved conflicts, all parts of your shadow self that need attention.

While dreams can range from mundane to fantastical, nightmares typically invoke fear or distress. However, both can be equally informative. Nightmares can be direct manifestations of trauma or intense fears, demanding attention and healing, whereas more neutral or positive dreams might highlight areas of growth, success, or desire.

Some common dream symbols and their meanings:

- Water: Represents emotions. Calm water might suggest emotional balance, while turbulent water can indicate suppressed or overwhelming feelings.
- Flying: Often related to desires for freedom or escape, or a sense of empowerment.
- Falling: Can symbolize feelings of loss of control, fear of failure, or letting go.

Individual vs. Universal Symbols: While some symbols, like water or flying, are commonly found across cultures and individuals, dream symbols are deeply personal. A snake might represent danger to one person and transformation to another.

HOW LONG SHOULD YOU ENGAGE IN DREAM ANALYSIS?

There's no one-size-fits-all. It might be weeks; for others, it could span months or even years. The journey of self-discovery is deeply personal. However, consistency in recording and analyzing dreams will undoubtedly deepen your understanding over time.

Dream analysis is a deeply personal journey, and its duration varies from person to person. Here are some points to consider:

- **Consistency is Key:** It's more beneficial to analyze dreams consistently over time rather than in intense, short bursts. A dream journal can be instrumental in tracking patterns over weeks or months.
- **Personal Comfort:** Engage in dream analysis as long as it feels productive and enlightening. If it becomes distressing or obsessive, it might be time to take a break or seek professional guidance.
- **Depth of Exploration:** Some dreams might be simple and need minimal analysis, while others might require deeper

introspection. It's essential to give each dream the time it deserves, which can vary.

- **Professional Guidance:** If you're continuously dealing with distressing dreams or can't make sense of recurring patterns, it might be helpful to consult a professional dream analyst or therapist.

Things to Expect:

- **Surprising Revelations:** Dreams can bring to light things you've long forgotten or suppressed.
- **Emotional Roller-coaster:** Some dreams might elicit strong emotional responses. It's okay; embrace and process them.
- **Evolution Over Time:** As you tackle issues and grow, your dream themes might change, reflecting your inner journey.

STEP-BY-STEP PROCESS

1. Document Your Dreams:

Why? The dream's essence often fades fast. Capturing it immediately preserves its purity.

How? Keep a dedicated dream journal and a pen on your nightstand. As soon as you wake up—even if it's in the middle of the night—write down as much as you can recall. Note the emotions, colors, people, settings, and even the weather.

Pro Tip: If you're not a writer, consider a voice recorder.

2. Analyze Symbols:

Why? Symbols are the language of dreams. They encapsulate complex emotions, situations, or memories in tangible forms.

How? For each symbol, ask yourself, "What does this mean to me?" A dog might symbolize loyalty to one and fear to another. There's no universal answer; it's deeply personal.

Pro Tip: Reference dream dictionaries, but always prioritize your personal associations.

3. Seek Patterns:

Why? Recurring themes or characters can be significant indicators of unresolved issues or pivotal life aspects.

How? Regularly review your dream journal. Are certain symbols or emotions making repeated appearances? Is there a specific setting you find yourself in often?

Pro Tip: Use colored highlighters to mark recurring themes. This visual aid can help in identifying patterns quickly.

4. Reflect:

Why? Introspection binds the whole process together, turning insights into actionable growth.

How? After analyzing, take a moment to sit with the dream. How does it make you feel? Can you relate it to any current life situation or a past memory?

Pro Tip: Sharing dreams with a trusted friend or therapist can provide additional perspectives. Sometimes, an external viewpoint can uncover angles you hadn't considered.

Quick overview & recap:

- **Recollection and Recording:** As soon as you wake, record your dream.

- **Identifying Core Symbols and Emotions:** Look for recurring images, characters, or emotions in the dream narrative.
- **Relating Dream Content to Waking Life:** Consider any recent events, feelings, or conflicts that might relate to the dream.
- **Reflecting on Personal Significance:** Think about how the dream makes you feel and what it reveals about your subconscious desires, fears, or traumas.

ETHICS AND BOUNDARIES IN DREAM SHARING AND ANALYSIS

Recognizing Our Own Biases and Projections: When interpreting someone else's dream, it's vital to be aware of and set aside our personal biases, ensuring we're not projecting our own experiences or beliefs onto them.

The Risks of Over-Analyzing or Over-Interpreting: Dreams are complex, and not every element needs or even has a definitive interpretation. Pressing for meanings where there might be none can cause unnecessary distress or confusion.

As you learn more about yourself and your shadow, dreams can serve as powerful allies, offering insights, revelations, and pathways to deeper self-understanding. However, as with all introspective work, it's essential to proceed with patience, compassion, and a genuine desire for growth and healing.

Diving into shadow work using dream analysis can be deeply transformative but also intense. So let's look at executing the advice with patience, compassion, and a genuine desire for growth and healing:

1. Set Clear Intentions

Step: Before you sleep, take a few moments to set an intention to remember your dreams. This intention can be as simple as saying to yourself, "I will remember my dreams tonight."

Tip: Keep a dream journal and pen by your bedside to show your subconscious you're serious about recording and analyzing your dreams.

2. Cultivate a Calm Sleeping Environment

Step: Ensure your sleeping space is quiet, dark, and comfortable. This not only aids better sleep but can also encourage more vivid dreaming.

Tip: Consider using calming essential oils like lavender, or listening to soft, ambient sounds to facilitate deeper sleep and dreams.

3. Record Dreams Immediately Upon Waking

Step: Write down everything you remember as soon as you wake up, even if it's just fragments or feelings.

Tip: If you struggle to recall dreams, jot down the very first emotion or image that comes to your mind upon waking. With time, your recall should improve.

4. Be Patient with Analysis

Step: When reviewing your dream journal, avoid rushing to conclusions. Take time to reflect on the emotions, symbols, and scenarios.

Tip: Sometimes, stepping away and revisiting a dream later can offer fresh insights. Your initial emotional response might cloud certain interpretations.

5. Embrace Compassion

Step: Some dreams may bring up uncomfortable emotions or memories. Approach them with self-compassion, acknowledging your feelings without judgment.

Tip: Remember that dreams are a safe space where your subconscious is communicating with you. Even if the messages are challenging, they come with a purpose of healing and growth.

6. Seek External Guidance When Needed

Step: If you're feeling stuck or overwhelmed, consider seeking guidance from a dream analyst, therapist, or trusted mentor.

Tip: Books on dream symbols can provide general interpretations, but always trust your intuition. Your personal associations with symbols are paramount.

7. Relate Dreams to Current Life Events

Step: Reflect on recent events, feelings, or conflicts in your waking life. Do they connect with your dreams in any way?

Tip: Consider using a mind map. Place your dream in the center and branch out to various aspects of your life. This visual representation can reveal connections.

8. Engage in Regular Self-Reflection

Step: Dedicate time each week to sit with your dream journal and reflect on patterns, recurring symbols, or emotions.

Tip: Pair this with meditation or deep breathing exercises to create a deeper connection with your subconscious.

9. Remember the Journey is Ongoing

Step: Shadow work and dream analysis aren't one-off tasks. Embrace them as ongoing processes in your journey towards self-awareness and healing.

Tip: Celebrate small revelations and victories along the way. This will motivate you to continue.

Dear reader, dreams are more than just fleeting images of the night. They're messages, advice, warnings, and stories from a part of you that doesn't always get to speak. Are you ready to listen?

9

ACTIVE IMAGINATION: A DIALOGUE WITH THE DEEP SELF

What if you could directly converse with the characters of your mind's theatre? What if, instead of being a passive observer, you actively engage with the symbols, stories, and scenarios your mind conjures? This is the realm of active imagination—a technique where the boundaries of reality and imagination blur, revealing the contours of our inner world.

WHAT IS ACTIVE IMAGINATION?

Active imagination is an explorative technique, championed by Jung, where one delves into their unconscious in a waking state. Unlike passive daydreaming, it's a deliberate and interactive process, allowing direct dialogue with the psyche's contents. It's like walking into a living dream and having a heart-to-heart with its inhabitants. Imagine!

Benefits include:

- Bridging Conscious and Unconscious: Facilitates communication between the two realms, fostering understanding and integration.
- Problem-Solving: Offers fresh perspectives on persistent life issues or challenges.
- Creativity Boost: An endless well for artists, writers, and creatives, tapping into original ideas and insights.

Who's Best Suited for Active Imagination?

Anyone can embark on this journey. However, it's especially beneficial if you:

- Are creatively inclined and seek inspiration.
- Feel disconnected and yearn for a dialogue with your inner self.
- Are curious about the intricate dance of symbols and stories within you.

How Long Should You Engage in Active Imagination?

Each session can last anywhere from a few minutes to an hour, depending on your comfort. It's not about the duration but the depth. It's a practice you can integrate into your life, returning to it whenever you seek inner guidance.

Start with 10 minutes, practice for 4 sessions, and increase by 5-10 minutes every 4 sessions you have. This way, you gradually increase your time spent within active imagination.

Things to Expect:

- **Surprising Interactions:** Your mind can conjure characters or scenarios you might not have consciously thought about.

- **Emotional Intensity:** Some sessions can be profoundly moving or even unsettling. Remember, it's a safe space to explore.
- **Evolving Narratives:** As you engage more, stories may evolve, reflecting your growth and understanding.

STEP-BY-STEP PROCESS

1. Find a Quiet Space:

Why? A distraction-free environment allows for deeper immersion.

How? Choose a place where you won't be interrupted—a cozy corner, a serene park, or even a silent room.

Pro Tip: Consider dim lighting or soft instrumental music to set the mood.

2. Close Your Eyes and Let Your Mind Wander:

Why? To invite the unconscious content forward without the conscious mind's strict filtering.

How? Sit or lie comfortably, take a few deep breaths, and let go. Trust your mind to guide the journey.

Pro Tip: If your mind feels too cluttered, a few minutes of meditation beforehand can help.

3. Engage with Your Imagination:

Why? Interaction deepens the experience, converting passive images to active insights. .

How? If a character or scenario arises, don't just watch. Interact. Ask questions. Seek clarity. Be genuinely curious.

Pro Tip: Embrace whatever arises, even if it seems bizarre or unrelated. Your psyche has its reasons.

4. Document the Experience:

Why? Capturing the essence aids reflection and helps trace your evolutionary journey over time.

How? After the session, while the experience is still fresh, jot down your encounters, emotions, and insights.

Pro Tip: Some find sketching or painting their experiences to be more expressive than words. Use whatever medium resonates.

My friend, active imagination is a potent tool in the arsenal of self-discovery. It's a bridge to the vast landscapes of your psyche, awaiting exploration. Remember, it's not about controlling the narrative but understanding it.

10

GUIDED MEDITATIONS & VISUALIZATIONS

Picture this: diving into the deep recesses of your mind, but not alone. With you is a trusted guide, leading you through the intricate pathways, ensuring you confront the right doors, the right shadows. This is the essence of guided meditations and visualizations—a structured journey into the unconscious with a voice leading the way.

WHAT ARE GUIDED MEDITATIONS AND VISUALIZATIONS?

They are structured meditation exercises, often led by an expert's voice, specifically tailored to navigate specific aspects of one's inner world. It's not just about relaxation; it's about revelation.

This method is useful for beginners because of the:

- Structured approach: Perfect for beginners or those who struggle to meditate on their own. The guide provides a roadmap.

- Targeted exploration: Tailored for specific purposes like shadow work, they direct attention where it's most needed.
- Safety net: For those wary of delving into their shadows, a guiding voice provides comfort and assurance.

Who's Best Suited for Guided Meditations?

While anyone can benefit, they're especially fruitful if you:

- Are new to meditation and desire structure.
- Want to target specific areas of self-exploration but aren't sure how.
- Seek the reassurance of a guiding presence in your inward journeys.

How Long Should You Engage in Guided Meditations?

Meditations can range from a quick 10-minute dive to more prolonged, hour-long sessions. Choose what fits your schedule and comfort. Regular practice, even if brief, can yield profound insights over time.

Things to Expect:

- **Emotional Surges:** As you confront your shadows, expect to feel a gamut of emotions.
- **Unexpected Revelations:** Even if you've meditated before, guided versions can lead to uncharted territories.
- **Deep Relaxation:** Beyond introspection, they often bring profound relaxation and clarity.

STEP-BY-STEP PROCESS

1. Choose a Meditation:

Why? Different guides offer varied journeys. Picking one aligned with your goals ensures a more meaningful experience.

How? Explore platforms like YouTube, meditation apps, or websites. Look for those explicitly focused on shadow work.

Pro Tip: Before settling on one, listen to a snippet. Ensure the guide's voice and style resonate with you.

2. Relax and Listen:

Why? Being fully present amplifies the experience.

How? Find a comfortable spot, use headphones for immersion, close your eyes, and let yourself be led.

Pro Tip: If distractions arise, gently bring your focus back to the guide's voice.

3. Engage with What Arises:

Why? Confrontation breeds clarity. Running away denies growth.

How? If feelings, memories, or insights surface, don't resist. Embrace, inquire, and understand.

Pro Tip: It's okay to feel overwhelmed. Take deep breaths and remember, it's a safe exploration.

4. Reflect Afterwards:

Why? Processing seals the insights and prepares you for the next step of your journey.

How? After the meditation, stay in silence for a few minutes, journal your feelings, or discuss them with a trusted person.

Pro Tip: Regular reflection deepens self-awareness. Over time, patterns may emerge, pointing to deeper truths.

Dear reader, consider guided meditations as a GPS for your soul's journey. They aren't just about relaxation; they're about revelation and regeneration. Are you prepared to let a guiding voice illuminate your shadows?

The reason why I'd recommend you go onto YouTube and other sources is because I know that every single person is different and this is a deeply personal journey for you. You have to find what works best for you and what you really like. You have to find the meditation that just feels right for you.

And unfortunately, it's not universal. It's personal to you.

However, what I will leave you with is a specific guided meditation that is simple to follow and an excellent starting point for beginners.

GUIDED MEDITATION FOR SHADOW WORK, TRAUMA, AND HEALING

Before starting this meditation, ensure you're in a comfortable, quiet space where you won't be disturbed. This meditation is about creating a safe space to face, understand, and integrate the shadows. Always such meditations with an open mind and heart.

1. Setting the Environment:

Dim the lights or light a soft candle.

Sit comfortably, either on a chair with feet flat on the ground or cross-legged on a cushion.

Ensure your spine is straight to allow for clear energy flow.

SHADOW WORK DEEP DIVE JOURNAL | 111

2. Breathing and Grounding (2 minutes):

Close your eyes and take a deep breath in through your nose, hold for a few seconds, then exhale slowly through your mouth.

Repeat this several times, feeling any tension in your body start to melt away.

Visualize roots extending from the base of your spine or your feet, going deep into the earth, grounding you.

3. Protective Shield (2 minutes):

Imagine a bright, warm light at the center of your chest, radiating outward.

This light expands, forming a protective bubble around you. Within this shield, you are safe, protected, and loved.

4. Journey to the Inner Sanctuary (3 minutes):

Visualize a pathway in a serene forest. Birds are chirping, and the leaves rustle gently in the wind.

Follow this pathway, feeling the cool earth beneath your feet.

The path leads to a clearing with a tranquil pool. This is your inner sanctuary, a safe space for introspection and healing.

5. Meeting Your Shadow (5 minutes):

As you stand by the pool, invite any shadow aspects or past traumas to come forward. This is a space of love, understanding, and healing.

See these shadows manifest as clouded reflections in the pool. Observe them without judgment, just curiosity.

Ask them: "What lessons do you hold for me? Why are you here?"

Listen intently, allowing memories, emotions, or insights to arise.

6. Embracing and Healing (4 minutes):

Breathe deeply, and with every exhale, release any pain, anger, or negative emotions tied to these shadows.

With every inhale, imagine golden, healing light filling those voids.

Slowly, lean down to touch the water's surface. As you do, visualize the clouded reflections starting to clear, turning into a brighter, calmer reflection.

7. Words of Affirmation (2 minutes):

Speak to your shadow: "Thank you for the lessons. I acknowledge you. I am ready to heal and move forward."

Feel a sense of gratitude and release.

8. Return to Conscious Awareness (2 minutes):

Gradually, begin retracing your steps back through the forest pathway.

As you walk, feel lighter, more integrated, and whole.

When ready, start to wiggle your fingers and toes, bringing awareness back to your physical surroundings.

9. Closing:

Place your hands over your heart, taking a moment to appreciate the journey you've embarked upon.

Take one deep breath, absorbing all the healing and understanding.

Open your eyes when you feel ready.

Note: This meditation can be deeply transformative, but also intense. Always make sure to hydrate and take it easy after the session. If you encounter particularly challenging or troubling memories or emotions, consider seeking professional support or therapy to assist in the healing process. Remember, you're not alone in your journey.

11

JOURNALING: UNFILTERED CONVERSATION WITH THE SELF

I magine if there was a mirror that not only reflected your face but the intricate weave of emotions, memories, and aspirations within you. Journaling, dear reader, is that mirror. It's an intimate dance between your thoughts and the page, each word echoing the rhythm of your soul. It really is that deep.

WHAT IS JOURNALING?

At its core, journaling is a dialogue with oneself, captured in writing. Unlike fleeting thoughts, these written words stay, echoing back insights, emotions, and patterns over time.

It's important for shadow work for reasons such as:

- **Self-reflection:** As you pen down your thoughts, you're also sifting through them, bringing clarity.
- **Safety:** It's a judgment-free zone. Just you and your words.
- **Documentation:** Over time, it becomes a repository of your emotional growth and transformations.

Who's Best Suited for Journaling?

Honestly, anyone. Whether you're:

- A seasoned writer or someone who's barely penned a diary entry.
- Someone seeking clarity or just a space to vent.
- Looking for patterns in behavior or just jotting down daily experiences.

How Long Should One Engage in Journaling?

It's flexible. Spend ten minutes a day or an hour once a week—whatever feels organic. The magic isn't in the duration but the consistency and authenticity.

Things to Expect:

- **Catharsis:** Releasing suppressed emotions can be incredibly therapeutic.
- **Surprising Insights:** Often, you'll find the pen revealing things your conscious mind hadn't acknowledged.
- **Emotional Swings:** Some days, your journal might be filled with joy, other days with tears or frustration. And that's perfectly okay.

STEP-BY-STEP PROCESS

1. Dedicate Time:

Why? Consistency amplifies the benefits.

How? Carve out a specific time daily or weekly. Make it a ritual—your sacred 'me' time.

Pro Tip: Even if you're not in the mood, just write about your day. Sometimes, the most mundane observations can lead to profound insights.

2. Write Freely:

Why? Authenticity is key. The journal is your safe space.

How? Start writing without overthinking. If it comes to your mind, it goes on the page.

Pro Tip: If you're stuck, begin with "Right now, I feel..."

3, Ask Yourself Questions:

Why? It prompts deeper introspection.

How? When recalling events or emotions, be inquisitive. Seek the 'why' behind your feelings.

Pro Tip: Remember, it's not about finding immediate answers. It's about asking the right questions.

4. Revisit Old Entries:

Why? The past often offers insights for the present.

How? Periodically, go back and read your older musings. Observe patterns, growth, or recurring themes.

Pro Tip: Date each entry. It helps track your emotional and psychological journey over time.

In the end, journaling is much more than a chronicle of daily life. It's a chronicle of growth, of self-awareness, of confronting and embracing your shadows.

In the same way, mediation is deeply personal. The same goes for journaling. So it's about exploring different exercises that resonate and work best for you.

With that being said, here's a great starting point.

Materials needed:

- A dedicated journal or notebook
- A pen that feels comfortable to write with
- A quiet, safe space where you can be undisturbed

EXERCISE STEPS

1. **Setting Intentions:** Begin by writing today's date at the top of a fresh page. Underneath, write the following affirmation: "I am open to understanding and healing my shadows. I embark on this journey with compassion, courage, and hope."
2. **Breathing and Grounding:** Before diving in, close your eyes and take three deep breaths, grounding yourself in the present moment. When you're ready, pen in hand, move to the next step.
3. **Identifying Shadows:** Think of a recent situation where you had a strong, perhaps unexpected, emotional reaction. Describe the event and your feelings.
4. **Reflecting on Origins:** Can you recall an earlier time in your life when you felt similarly? Often, our intense reactions stem from past events or patterns. Dive into your memories. What do they reveal?
5. **The Message Behind the Shadow:** What might this shadowy emotion or reaction be trying to tell you or teach you? Is there a hidden message or lesson behind this feeling?
6. **Confronting Fears:** List three fears or negative beliefs that this shadow might be anchored to. For each fear, write down a positive affirmation to counteract it. For example, if a fear

is "I am unlovable," the counter affirmation could be "I am worthy of love and belonging."

7. **Dream Exploration (optional):** Have you had any recent dreams that resonate with this shadow or emotion? Describe the dream and any feelings or insights it brought up.

8. **Steps Toward Healing:** Identify three small actions or changes you can make in your daily life to acknowledge and heal this shadow. This could be a new daily affirmation, setting boundaries, seeking therapy, or any other positive step.

9. **Gratitude and Light:** While shadow work can be intense, it's also an act of self-love. Write down three things you're grateful for right now. They can be related to this journey or simply joys in your life.

10. **Closing Reflection:** How do you feel after this journaling session? Imagine a future where you've fully integrated and healed this shadow. What does that look like? How does that version of you feel?

12

NAVIGATING CHALLENGES AND ROADBLOCKS

As with any great expedition, the journey into our shadows is not without its challenges. At times, the road is paved and clear; other times, it's riddled with boulders and pitfalls. But remember this: the shadows may be deep and vast, but the light within you is stronger.

COMMON CHALLENGES IN THE SHADOW JOURNEY

1. Resistance: The Pushback of the Psyche

Think of resistance as a protective older sibling, albeit sometimes overprotective. It's trying to shield you from the pain of the past. But, as you might already know, to heal, sometimes we need to feel. Our brain are naturally wired for survival. When confronted with distressing memories or thoughts, its natural instinct is to push them away to maintain our well-being.

Recognizing Resistance:

- Physical Signs: A tightening in the chest, shallow breathing, or a sudden urge to get up and do something else.
- Mental Signs: Thoughts like "Why am I even doing this?" or a persistent urge to switch focus.
- Emotional Signs: Feeling irritable, anxious, or excessively drained post introspection.
- How It Might Manifest in Your Life: You might find yourself starting shadow work, then abruptly stopping, time and time again. Or avoiding certain topics entirely.

Resistance is a sign you're touching something significant. Instead of fighting it, thank it for its protection and assure your mind that you're safe and ready to face what's been buried.

2. Fear: Facing the Monsters in the Closet

The shadows house our insecurities, past traumas, and deep-seated fears. And let's be honest, who truly enjoys facing their monsters? It's human nature to fear what we don't understand or what has hurt us in the past.

Recognizing fear:

- Physical Signs: Goosebumps, a racing heart, or a sudden cold feeling.
- Mental Signs: Dread or constant apprehension when thinking about diving deep.
- Emotional Signs: A feeling of being trapped or overwhelmed.
- How It Might Manifest in Your Life: Maybe you avoid certain places, songs, or movies because they evoke strong negative emotions. That's your shadow, gently nudging you.

Instead of diving headfirst, take it step by step. Face smaller fears first, building your confidence to confront bigger ones.

3. Denial: The Illusive Veil

Denial, in essence, is a safety blanket. But to grow, we must learn to fly solo and lose the stabilizers. Acknowledging our shadows means acknowledging our flaws, past mistakes, and vulnerabilities. And sometimes, that's just tough!

Recognizing denial:

- Physical Signs: An instinctive shake of the head or a shrug when confronted with certain truths.
- Mental Signs: Thoughts like "That's not like me" or "I would never do that".
- Emotional Signs: Feeling defensive or angry when someone points out certain behaviors.
- How It Might Manifest in Your Life: Perhaps you've heard feedback, both from life and loved ones, about certain behaviors but always brushed it off.

Self-compassion is the key thing here. Remind yourself that recognizing a shadow isn't admitting to being 'bad' or 'wrong'. It's about understanding yourself fully and fostering growth. Journeying into our shadows isn't just about facing the dark; it's about finding the light that's been obscured by it. Each challenge is a signpost that you're on the right path. After all, no great adventure is without its trials, and what greater adventure is there than understanding oneself?

It's absolutely natural to feel overwhelmed at times. The path into our innermost recesses can be treacherous. But how do we navigate this so that shadow work can be seen through to the end and used to its fullest?

OVERCOMING CHALLENGES

1. Take Breathers: The Art of Pausing

Your mind and emotions are muscles. Like any muscle, they can get tired. By pausing, you give them a chance to rest and rejuvenate.

If you start feeling overwhelmed, agitated, or even physically fatigued, that's your inner self signaling for a timeout. Don't be afraid to take a break when you know you need it.

For me, I like to find a peaceful spot, engage in an activity that calms you which for me is playing the guitar. But be it reading, taking a walk, or just napping. Listen to calming music, practice deep breathing, or even indulge in a hobby. The key is to momentarily shift focus.

2. Seek Support: The Power of Community

You know how in movies, the protagonist always has that one buddy or mentor they lean on? It's not just a cinematic trope. We all need our 'squad'. Hey, maybe we've just uncovered another archetype! Humans are social beings. Sometimes, just voicing your fears and anxieties can be cathartic.

Who to Reach Out To:

- Friends & Family: Those who know you best might offer insights you hadn't considered.
- Professionals: Therapists and counselors are trained to guide people through their inner mazes.
- Support Groups: These are communities of fellow travelers on the same journey. They provide a safe space to share and learn from others' experiences.
- Start with a simple, "I need to talk." Remember, vulnerability is a strength.

3. Focus on the Bigger Picture: Your 'Why'

The path might be rugged and the weather stormy, but there's a reason you set out on this journey.

The importance of your 'why' cannot be understated. Your purpose is your compass. When lost, it'll guide you back.

How to reconnect with your purpose:

- Reflection: Sit quietly and remind yourself of the moment you decided to start this journey. What ignited that spark?
- Visualize: Picture the healed, integrated version of yourself. How does it feel to be that person?
- Affirmations: Create personal mantras that resonate with your purpose. Repeat them, especially during challenging moments.
- Visualising: Create a vision board, journal about your progress, or even discuss your goals with someone you trust. Keep your destination in sight.

No explorer ever said their journey was easy. But they all agree on one thing—it was worth it. Whenever you feel like the weight's too heavy, come back to these tools. They're your trusty companions in this grand adventure. Onward, explorer!

13

THE CONCEPT OF GROUNDING

ANCHORING YOURSELF TO THE PRESENT

You're a ship, floating through the vast ocean of your emotions and memories. Now, every ship, no matter how grand or small, needs an anchor to stabilize it, especially during storms. Grounding, in essence, is that anchor for your emotional and mental state. It's the process of connecting with the present moment, anchoring yourself to the here and now, especially after venturing deep into the waters of your psyche.

At its core, grounding helps you distinguish between the emotional intensity of past experiences and the reality of the current moment. Think of it as a gentle reminder that, even after delving into the recesses of your shadows, you're still here, safe and whole, in the present.

TECHNIQUES FOR GROUNDING: YOUR EMOTIONAL
TOOLKIT

Have you ever felt like a leaf, caught up in a gust of wind, swept from
one emotional whirlwind to another? It's not an uncommon sensa-
tion, especially when diving deep into personal reflections and
shadow work. But, what if you had a tool, a method to anchor yourself amidst these gusts, to feel solid ground beneath your feet once
more? Enter the world of grounding techniques. These simple, yet
powerful practices can be your lifeline, pulling you back into the
embrace of the present moment.

1. Visualization: The Imaginary Anchor

Visualization is a potent tool. Our minds are incredibly adept at
crafting intricate images and scenarios. And in grounding, we
harness this power to establish stability and presence.

- The Rooted Tree Technique: Imagine, if you will, that you
  are a massive tree. Your feet are the roots, digging deep into
  the nurturing earth. With every inhale, feel the energy of the
  earth rising, stabilizing you. And with every exhale, let go of
  any lingering tension. You, like the tree, are grounded, firm,
  and unshakeable.
- The Safe Space Technique: Think of a place where you've felt
  utterly calm and secure. It could be a childhood home, a
  serene beach, or even a fictional haven. When you feel
  scattered, transport yourself to this place in your mind.
  Explore its nooks and crannies, and embrace the safety it
  offers.

Did you know? Many individuals claim that frequent visualization
not only aids in grounding but also sharpens the mind's imaginative
capabilities. It's like a gym workout for your brain!

2. Physical Exercises: Engaging the Body to Calm the Mind

There's a unique connection between our bodies and our emotional states. Physical grounding techniques use this link to bring about a sense of calm and presence.

- Barefoot Walks: There's something intrinsically grounding about feeling the earth beneath our feet. Whenever you're overwhelmed, consider a short walk on grass or sand. Feel the textures, the temperature, and let nature's touch ground you.
- Progressive Muscle Relaxation: Starting from your toes and working up to your head, tense each muscle group for a few seconds and then release. This conscious engagement with each part of your body brings immediate awareness and presence.
- Personal Touch: Emily, a seasoned yoga practitioner, often emphasized the importance of the 'Mountain Pose' or 'Tadasana' for grounding. The act of standing firm, feeling every part of the foot on the ground, and visualizing oneself as an immovable mountain was a favorite technique of hers to instill a deep sense of calm.

3. Sensory Awareness: Embracing the Here and Now

Our senses—sight, smell, touch, taste, and sound—are gateways to the present. Engaging them is a direct route back to the here and now.

- The 5-4-3-2-1 Technique: This simple exercise involves identifying five things you can see, four you can touch, three you can hear, two you can smell, and one you can taste. It's a swift and efficient method to pull your awareness back to your current environment.

- Aromatic Anchors: Scents have a profound ability to evoke memories and emotions. However, they can also anchor us. Consider keeping a vial of a grounding scent, like cedarwood or sandalwood, close by. A deep inhalation during overwhelming moments can work wonders.

Always remember, dear reader, that it's okay if one technique resonates more than another. Your grounding journey is uniquely yours. Find what feels right, what soothes your soul, and embrace it. The ultimate goal is to find your way back to the present, to stand firm amidst the ever-shifting sands of emotions and memories. It wouldn't actually be beneficial for you to be actively practising all of these techniques equally, as you simply don't need them all at once, they are all different paths to the same outcome. That's not to say you can't use multiple in conjunction, or even combine some together if it works for you. The bottom line is more focus on the ones that resonate most with you, will not only feel better but also be more effective.

YOUR GROUNDING COMPASS

In the explorative journey of shadow work, it's easy to lose one's way. But with grounding, you've got a compass, always pointing back to the present, to the tangible now. Each time you feel adrift, know that these techniques are your North Star, guiding you back to the safety of the shore. Remember, in this journey, you're never truly alone; grounding is always by your side.

14

THE SIGNIFICANCE OF SELF-COMPASSION IN SHADOW WORK

UNDERSTANDING SELF-COMPASSION: BEYOND MERE KINDNESS

Have you ever sat beside a still pond, watching ripples form with every pebble thrown? Now, imagine your mind as that pond. Every judgment, every harsh word, sends ripples through, disturbing the calm. Self-compassion, dear reader, is the art of ensuring the pond remains undisturbed, serene.

Self-compassion isn't just about offering ourselves platitudes of kindness. It delves deeper. It's about granting ourselves the understanding, patience, and acceptance we'd offer to a dear friend. It's recognizing that, like everyone else, we're human—fallible, imperfect, yet wholly deserving of love and kindness. Dr. Kristin Neff, a prominent voice in this realm, describes it as comprising three elements: self-kindness, shared humanity, and mindfulness. Together, these form the bedrock of genuine self-compassion.

WHY IT'S CRUCIAL IN SHADOW WORK

Diving into the murky waters of our psyche is no easy feat. There will be times during your shadow work journey when you'll uncover memories, emotions, or traits that may feel uncomfortable or even painful. This is natural. After all, shadows are parts of us we've often tucked away because they were too overwhelming to face.

However, imagine doing this challenging work while being your harshest critic. Without self-compassion, you might be tempted to label yourself: "Why was I so naive?" or "How could I have been so selfish?" This blame game, laden with guilt or resentment, doesn't facilitate healing. It merely deepens wounds.

Now, let's flip the script. Approach these revelations with under-standing and kindness. Instead of blame, there's empathy. Instead of resentment, understanding. That, dear reader, is the magic of self-compassion. It acts as a buffer, ensuring that as you confront your shadows, you do so with a nurturing, healing intent. Instead of being a process of self-flagellation, shadow work becomes an intimate dance of self-understanding. Here are some steps for self compassion.

SELF-REFLECTION: THE POWER OF PAUSE

Do you remember the last time you stubbed your toe and blurted out, "I'm so clumsy!"? We all have those moments of self-judgment. They come easily, almost reflexively. But what if, instead of immedi-ately defaulting to criticism, we paused?

Imagine that brief moment as a bridge—a bridge between impulse and response. By introducing self-reflection, you give yourself the opportunity to cross that bridge mindfully. When those harsh words or judgments arise, challenge them. Ask yourself: "Would I speak to my best friend like this?". Pausing, reflecting, and shifting that narrative is the first, crucial step to cultivate self-compassion. Think of it as adjusting your internal compass, steering it towards kindness and understanding.

DAILY AFFIRMATIONS: YOUR INTERNAL CHEERLEADER

Ever caught yourself humming a catchy tune hours after you heard it? Affirmations work in a similar way; they're like catchy, positive tunes for your mind. Repeated often enough, they start to change your internal dialogue.

Let's try it. Instead of "I'm not good enough," how about "I am worthy and deserving"? Rather than "I can't handle this," try "I am resilient, and I grow with every challenge."

Here are a few affirmations to sprinkle into your day:

- "I am a work in progress, and that's okay."
- "I give myself permission to make mistakes and learn from them."
- "Every day, I grow stronger in self-love and understanding."

Choose one. Say it out loud. Better yet, say it to yourself in the mirror. Feel the shift.

MINDFUL MEDITATION: A RETURN TO THE SELF

There's a quiet place within all of us, away from the hustle and bustle of daily life. Mindful meditation offers a pathway to this sanctuary. This isn't about achieving some transcendent state but about grounding oneself, becoming aware of the present, and truly listening to one's inner world.

Start simply. Find a quiet spot. Close your eyes and focus on your breathing. Feel the rise and fall of your chest, the cool air entering, the warm air leaving. When your mind wanders (and it will), gently bring it back to the breath. Even just five minutes a day of this practice can heighten your self-awareness and, in turn, your capacity for self-compassion.

PRACTICE GRATITUDE: THE LENS OF APPRECIATION

When storms brew within, it's challenging to see the silver linings. Gratitude, dear reader, offers a fresh perspective. By consciously focusing on things to be thankful for, we not only shift our viewpoint but also make room for self-compassion.

Try this: at the end of each day, jot down three things you're grateful for. It could be a warm meal, a kind word, or simply the air you breathe. Over time, this practice not only fosters positivity but also a gentle understanding of the self, enhancing our ability to be compassionate.

THE LINK BETWEEN SELF-AWARENESS AND SELF-COMPASSION

Have you ever stared at your reflection, truly stared, and wondered about the universe of emotions, thoughts, and stories behind those eyes? It's a deep dive, isn't it? That dive is the essence of self-awareness. It's a journey into the very fabric of who you are—your feelings, reactions, triggers, and desires.

Let's consider an analogy. Imagine your psyche as a vast mansion, with numerous rooms, some well-lit and others darkened by shadows. Self-awareness is like exploring this mansion, room by room, turning on the lights, and taking note of the contents. The brighter the rooms, the clearer you see, understand, and eventually, accept yourself.

Now, where does self-compassion fit in? It's the comforting presence, the gentle hand guiding you through this mansion, ensuring you don't get lost or overwhelmed. When you uncover painful memories or confront difficult emotions, self-compassion whispers, "It's okay. This is a part of you, and it's okay to feel this way."

THE CYCLE OF AWARENESS AND COMPASSION: AN EVER-GROWING SPIRAL

Picture this: a spiral, continuously evolving and expanding. At its core? Self-awareness and self-compassion. The two aren't just connected—they feed into each other, propelling you forward on your path of growth.

As you become more self-aware, recognizing and understanding your inner nuances, you naturally start to exercise greater self-compassion. You begin to treat yourself with the kindness and understanding you'd extend to a close friend. This compassion, in turn, encourages even deeper levels of self-awareness. It provides the safe space necessary for you to further explore your shadows and light. And so, the spiral grows.

Dear reader, understand this: this isn't a linear journey. It's a dance. Sometimes, you lead with self-awareness, and other times, compassion takes the lead. But together, they create a harmonious, enriching rhythm.

THE ROLE OF COMPASSION IN GROWTH: EMBRACING SHADOWS WITH OPEN ARMS

Every one of us has shadows—parts of ourselves that we've pushed away, ignored, or perhaps didn't even know existed. Confronting them can be daunting, even terrifying. But what if you approached them not as enemies, but as old friends waiting to be understood?

That's where self-compassion plays a pivotal role. When you treat yourself with compassion, you give yourself the permission to explore these shadows without the weight of judgment or fear. Instead of recoiling from what you find, you greet it with curiosity: "Why do I feel this way?" "What caused this reaction?" It's like giving yourself a comforting hug and assuring yourself that it's okay to be imperfect.

By doing so, you unlock deeper insights into yourself. This understanding fosters personal growth, helping you heal past wounds, release blocked energies, and integrate your shadows. The result? A more authentic, integrated, and compassionate version of yourself.

Imagine if, instead of treating your journey of self-discovery as a daunting trek, you viewed it as a reunion—a reconnection with all parts of yourself, both light and shadow. With self-awareness as your guide and self-compassion as your comforting companion, you can traverse this path with grace, patience, and profound understanding.

So, the next time you catch a glimpse of yourself in the mirror, pause. Know that behind those eyes lies a universe, waiting to be explored with kindness and compassion. Embrace it, for this journey, dear reader, is one of the most transformative you'll ever undertake.

SECTION 4

EMOTIONS: THE LANGUAGE OF THE
SHADOW

In a dimly lit concert hall, an orchestra readies itself. There's an air of anticipation. The audience – your conscious mind – settles into their seats, awaiting the performance. Your soul, acting as the conductor, raises the baton, and the music begins.

Now, imagine this orchestra as a metaphor for your inner emotional world. Each instrument represents a distinct emotion. The violin might echo the melancholic notes of sadness, while the trumpet blares with fiery anger. The flute gently flutters with joy, and the drums resonate with anxiety's heavy beats. Sometimes, the melody is a euphonious blend of contentment and hope; at other times, it's a cacophonous outburst of despair and rage.

But here's the thing: every note played, whether harmonious or discordant, holds meaning. Each emotion, every instrument, tells a tale about a hidden part of ourselves. They are not just random sounds in the vast auditorium of our minds. Rather, they're messages. Clues that hint towards deeper truths, unresolved conflicts, and shadows lurking in the backdrop.

In our journey of self-exploration and shadow work, understanding this orchestra becomes pivotal. For it's not just about listening to these melodies but interpreting them. Emotions, with their ebb and flow, serve as a compass, guiding us through the labyrinth of our psyche, leading us to the very shadows we seek to illuminate.

As we delve deeper into this section, think of yourself not just as an audience member but as an active participant, a musician even, ready to engage with, understand, and harmonize the varied tunes of your emotional world.

15

SIGNS AND SYMPTOMS: THE SHADOW'S WHISPERS

INTRODUCTION: UNMASKING THE HIDDEN SELF & TUNING IN TO THE SHADOW'S FREQUENCY

Imagine walking through a museum of mirrors, each reflecting not just your physical appearance, but facets of your inner self, some of which you're unfamiliar with or might have even forgotten. This is the realm of the shadow—parts of us that lurk just beneath the surface, occasionally emerging in unexpected ways. Recognizing these moments, these telltale signs, is the first step toward embracing and integrating our full selves. In this chapter, we'll delve into the various signals and tools that can help us identify our shadow.

It's important to note that just like a radio, trying to find a station. Amidst the static, there are moments when the music becomes clear, but only for a moment before getting lost again. Our shadow's signals are often like that—sometimes loud and distinct, other times muffled by our conscious mind's chatter. The key is to know what to listen for.

EMOTIONAL OUTBURSTS: THE UNEXPECTED WAVES

We've all been there—a casual comment from a friend or a slight change in plans, and suddenly, there's this inexplicable surge of emotion. Think of these outbursts as the alarm bells of the shadow.

Why It Happens: When an aspect of our shadow feels threatened or recognized, it reacts. It's like poking a sleeping beast. This isn't a sign of weakness or being 'too emotional'; it's a nudge from your deeper self saying, "Hey, there's something here you need to look at."

Situation 1: The Forgotten Coffee - On a seemingly average morning, your partner forgets to make you coffee. Instead of a fleeting moment of disappointment, you're overcome by a wave of anger and feelings of being invisible.

Situation 2: The Casual Feedback - During a work presentation, a colleague mildly critiques one of your points. Rather than taking it in stride, you're submerged in an overwhelming tide of inadequacy.

Situation 3: The Missed Call - Your friend misses one of your calls and doesn't call back immediately. Instead of considering their busy schedule, you're enveloped by a sense of rejection.

For The Introspective Soul: The magnitude of our reactions often carries clues. Is the reaction truly about the situation at hand, or is it echoing unresolved emotions from our past?

For You, The Explorer: The next time a minor event triggers a major reaction, ask yourself: "Why did this affect me so profoundly?" Dive deep. The answer might surprise you.

PROJECTION: MIRRORS EVERYWHERE

You know that irksome feeling when someone's actions or traits annoy you to no end, even if they're seemingly insignificant? Well, sometimes, what we dislike in others is what we've yet to accept in ourselves.

The Science Behind It: Jung believed that we project our shadows onto others. So, when someone becomes an intense source of irritation, they might be mirroring a part of our shadow back to us.

Situation 1: The Overconfident Peer - There's this team member who, in your eyes, always brags about their accomplishments. Deep down, could they be reflecting your suppressed desire for recognition?

Situation 2: The Adventurous Acquaintance - A friend constantly shares their adventurous escapades. Instead of joy, you feel annoyance. Perhaps they're mirroring a hidden longing for excitement in your life?

Situation 3: The 'Perfect' Neighbor - Your neighbor seems to have it all, and you can't help but nitpick their flaws. Could this be a manifestation of your internal struggle with self-acceptance?

A Nudge to Ponder: When our reactions to others feel disproportionately intense, it's often a sign they're revealing parts of us we haven't fully embraced.

A Guiding Question: The next time someone's behavior bothers you out of proportion, step back and reflect: "Is this something I see in myself? Is this a quality I've suppressed or denied?"

AVOIDANCE BEHAVIOR: DODGING THE SPOTLIGHT

Some topics, memories, or feelings make us so uncomfortable that we'd rather lock them in a mental box and throw away the key. This isn't mere forgetfulness; it's our psyche's way of saying, "I'm not ready to deal with this... yet."

Spotting Avoidance: It's when you change the topic quickly, or when memories are brushed off with a "let's not go there." It's the unease, the rapid heartbeat when certain subjects arise.

Situation 1: The Gathering Shift - At family reunions, when tales of past relationships arise, you suddenly feel the need to refill your drink or check on the food, consistently avoiding the topic.

Situation 2: The Evaded Song - A specific song plays on the radio, and you promptly switch stations every time, unable to pinpoint why it unnerves you.

Situation 3: The Skipped Book Chapter - You're engrossed in a book, but when it touches themes of childhood friendships, you find reasons to put it down, skimming or even skipping that section.

Gentle Wisdom: Avoidance isn't merely about dodging discomfort; it's the soul's way of pointing towards areas needing our attention and healing.

A Gentle Reminder: It's okay to have areas you're not ready to delve into. Remember, shadow work isn't a race. It's a journey, taken one step at a time, at a pace that's right for you.

JAKE'S REALIZATION

Jake was the punctual guy. The one who'd show up at meetings ten minutes early and judge anyone who was even a minute late. But one day, after snapping at a late colleague, he took a moment to introspect. Why did tardiness irk him so much? Delving deep, he remembered the younger Jake—a teenager who'd often been late, missing opportunities and facing scoldings. He had internalized this guilt, turning it into a shadow that equated punctuality with self-worth. Recognizing this was his first step toward understanding and, eventually, healing.

THE LANDSCAPE OF EMOTIONS

THE SPECTRUM OF SENSATIONS

Close your eyes and imagine yourself in an art gallery. As you move from one exhibit to another, you notice a vast collection of colors. Some shades are bright and vibrant, instantly catching your eye, while others are muted, soft, and often overlooked. Now, imagine these colors representing your emotions. The fiery reds of anger, the deep blues of sorrow, the radiant yellows of joy, and the subdued grays of indifference.

Our emotional palette is as varied and rich as these colors. From the highs of elation to the depths of despair, from the calm of contentment to the turbulence of jealousy, we have the capacity to feel a wide spectrum of emotions. Yet, society often labels them for us: happiness is "good," anger is "bad," contentment is "desired," and jealousy is "shameful."

However, in the realm of self-awareness and shadow work, such labels can be counterproductive. Emotions, in their purest form, are neutral. They are messengers, signaling something about our internal state, our needs, and our desires. It's our response, our reaction, and the meaning we ascribe to them that often casts them in a positive or negative light.

Grab a journal or just take a quiet moment for yourself. Think back to a time when you felt a surge of genuine contentment. Where were you? Who were you with? What sparked that emotion? Now, shift gears and recall a moment when jealousy took hold. Was it a fleeting feeling or did it linger? What triggered it? By engaging in this reflective exercise, you begin to chart your emotional landscape. You'll start to discern patterns, triggers, and most importantly, the shadows that might be influencing these emotions from behind the scenes.

Remember, it's not about judging these feelings or trying to suppress them. It's about understanding them. By recognizing and accepting every hue of your emotional spectrum, you're taking the first step in acknowledging the hidden facets of your psyche. And as any artist will tell you, even the most overlooked shades have a role to play in creating a masterpiece. In your case, it's the masterpiece of self-understanding and integration.

EMOTIONS AS GATEWAYS

Emotions, often described as fleeting and transient, are like ripples on the surface of a pond. While the ripple is evident, it's essential to remember that something beneath the water's surface created it. Similarly, our emotions are surface reactions to deeper internal dynamics. They can act as windows, providing glimpses into the often-hidden chambers of our psyche.

Consider emotions as keys. Each one has the potential to unlock a part of yourself you may not be fully aware of. When you feel an emotion, especially one that's strong or seems out of place, it's like a beacon flashing, signaling you to pay attention. Why is this emotion surfacing now? What is it trying to convey? What part of your past, which shadow, is trying to make itself heard?

This is where the introspective aspect of shadow work comes into play. Rather than shying away from these emotions or suppressing them, we should lean into them. We should ask ourselves questions, get curious, and gently probe to understand the root cause. By doing so, you're not just addressing the surface ripple; you're diving deep, reaching the very stone that caused it.

Elena grew up surrounded by friends who had siblings. At school, she'd hear tales of brotherly pranks, sisterly squabbles, and those unique bonds siblings shared. She'd laugh along, share in their joys and sorrows, but in her heart, there was always a twinge of something she couldn't quite place. Was it jealousy? Longing? Bitterness?

Every time she'd see siblings bonding, that pang would return, more pronounced. It was a feeling she couldn't shake off. Elena decided to sit with this emotion. Why did it affect her so? What was it trying to show her?

Upon reflection, she realized that her emotion was a doorway to a part of her she hadn't acknowledged. Being an only child wasn't just a fact of her life; it was a shadow that held layers of unexpressed feelings—loneliness during childhood games, longing for a sibling's protective presence, and the weight of being the sole focus of her parents' expectations.

By recognizing and exploring her emotion, Elena was not only able to identify her shadow but also to begin the process of embracing and integrating it. She started joining support groups for only children, sharing her feelings, and finding solace in shared experiences. What once was a source of pain became a path to healing and self-understanding.

Such is the power of emotions. They aren't just feelings; they're guideposts, leading you on a journey inward. All you have to do is be willing to follow their lead.

THE BOTTLENECK DILEMMA

If you've ever tried to pour a gallon of water through a narrow-necked bottle, you'd know the mess that ensues. The water overflows, splashes everywhere, and you're left with a puddle to clean. Our emotional reservoir is quite similar. When we continuously pour emotions into our being without a proper outlet, it's bound to overflow eventually, often in unexpected and sometimes harmful ways.

Suppressing emotions is akin to placing a tight lid on a pot of boiling water. For a while, the steam, under pressure, remains inside. But, given enough time and heat, that lid will either pop off, or the pot will crack. Similarly, when we deny ourselves the release of emotional expression, we're creating an internal pressure cooker.

Why do we suppress? Often, society, culture, or personal beliefs play a part. There's a certain image to maintain, certain expectations to meet. We're taught that some emotions are "unacceptable" or "weak". But by doing so, we're doing a disservice to our holistic well-being.

The consequences of emotional suppression aren't just mental or emotional. Physical health can be affected too—stress, high blood pressure, and even heart-related issues can be exacerbated by unexpressed emotions.

Growing up in a traditional household, James was often reminded of his role as the "man of the future family." Emotions, especially those deemed as vulnerable like sadness or fear, were seen as weaknesses. "Men don't cry," was a phrase he'd heard often, and over time, it became a part of his internal monologue. Every time he felt the sting of tears, whether from a scraped knee as a kid or a broken heart as a teen, he'd swallow down the lump in his throat, square his shoulders, and move on.

Years of this emotional bottling led James to become somewhat of a stoic. But bottled emotions, much like carbonated drinks, tend to fizz over eventually. One day, after a particularly long day at work, James found his takeaway order mixed up. A trivial issue, but it was the straw that broke the camel's back. He exploded at the restaurant staff, a whirlwind of pent-up anger, frustration, and tears.

It took that outburst for James to realize that his emotional reservoir was overflowing. It wasn't about the wrong food order; it was about years of suppressed feelings seeking an outlet. It was only later than James took a long, hard look at his emotional practices and decided to make changes that allowed him to feel, process, and express.

His journey wasn't smooth. There were times he'd falter, revert to old habits, but with time, patience, and understanding, James learned the importance of emotional expression. His relationships improved, his health stabilized, and he felt a sense of emotional freedom he'd never known.

The message here? Emotions are natural. They're a part of the human experience. Denying them is denying a part of ourselves. So, the next time you feel the urge to cry, laugh, scream, or dance, go ahead. Let it out. Embrace the full spectrum of your emotional being, and in doing so, embrace your authentic self.

EMOTIONAL CATHARSIS: TECHNIQUES AND TOOLS

There's a certain magic in release—a deep, profound sense of liberation when we let our emotions flow freely, untethered. But how do we navigate this release? How do we process emotions, especially when they come surging forth like a tidal wave, threatening to consume us? Just as a craftsman has the tools to mold his masterpiece, we too have techniques and practices that can assist us in shaping our emotional well-being.

Emotional Freedom Techniques (EFT): Also known as 'tapping,' EFT combines elements of cognitive therapy with acupressure. By tapping on specific meridian points while verbalizing our feelings, we can work towards releasing emotional blockages. It might sound unconventional, but countless individuals swear by its effectiveness in managing stress, anxiety, and emotional upheaval.

Did you know EFT has been used successfully by veterans and trauma survivors, helping them process and cope with their experiences?

Artistic Expression: Not all of us are wordsmiths, and that's okay. Emotion finds expression in myriad ways. Painting, sculpting, dancing, singing—choose your medium and let your soul speak. Artistic endeavors have a unique way of mirroring our innermost feelings, providing both a mirror and a release.

Anecdote: Maya was never good with words. When asked how she felt, she'd often draw a blank. But give her a canvas and paints, and she'd paint you a storm, a sunset, or a tranquil sea, each depicting her emotional state. Through colors and strokes, Maya found her voice.

Engage in a Freedom Write: Set aside your doubts, judgments, and hesitations for a moment. Grab a pen and paper. Set a timer for five minutes. Now, write. Don't think, don't pause, don't judge. Just let the words flow. Scribbles, doodles, sentences, or words—it doesn't matter. This is your canvas, and these are your emotions.

Once the timer goes off, take a deep breath. How do you feel? Lighter? Overwhelmed? Surprised? Reflect on this experience. You might find that amidst the chaos, there lie pearls of wisdom, insights into your emotional landscape that you might have overlooked.

Remember, processing emotions isn't a one-size-fits-all journey. It's deeply personal, ever-evolving. The tools and techniques are mere aids, guiding you towards your destination of emotional well-being. Embrace them, experiment with them, and find what resonates with you. The path to emotional catharsis is paved with patience, under-standing, and self-love. Step forth with an open heart and an eager soul, for the journey is as enlightening as the destination.

17

EMOTIONS AS INDICATORS OF DEEPER ISSUES

There's a reason the phrase 'tip of the iceberg' is so popular—it beautifully illustrates the unseen depths that lie beneath the surface. Think of emotions in a similar manner. What we often experience—the anger, joy, sadness, or frustration—is just the visible portion, the tip. Beneath that waterline, a colossal structure of past experiences, beliefs, traumas, and unfulfilled desires lurk, giving rise to those very emotions.

Picture that iceberg, floating serenely in an expanse of water. The peak is clearly visible, but as you dive deeper, the enormity becomes evident. This is your emotional self. The surface feelings are easy to spot, but the deeper elements require diving, exploring, and understanding.

The beauty of the iceberg analogy is its reminder that the surface, though important, is not the complete picture. Every fleeting emotion, every outburst, every moment of joy is rooted in something deeper. Recognizing this is the first step to genuine self-understanding.

DECODING EMOTIONAL PATTERNS

Life, in its infinite wisdom, has a way of offering us patterns, clues. Think of these as nature's way of nudging us, saying, "Hey, something's up. Pay attention." But how do we decipher these patterns?

- **Awareness:** Before understanding patterns, one needs to be aware of them. Keep an emotional log. Over time, you might see patterns emerge—a recurrent sense of inadequacy, bouts of unexplained anger, or perhaps consistent feelings of joy in specific situations.
- **Questioning:** Once a pattern is identified, be curious. Why do you always feel anxious before team meetings? Why does a casual comment from a loved one trigger sadness? By asking 'why,' we embark on a journey inwards.
- **Connection:** Link these patterns to events, past experiences, or unacknowledged desires. This step can be revelatory, often unearthing shadow elements that have long been ignored.

Tara was a beacon of confidence, always in control. Yet, every time someone was even slightly late, she'd be engulfed in an inexplicable feeling of abandonment. It wasn't about the tardiness, but the emotion it evoked. After introspection, Tara unearthed a deeply buried memory—watching through teary eyes as her father packed his bags and left, promising to return but never did. That child's feeling of abandonment had grown into an adult's shadow. An adult shadow that was triggering intense emotions even in mundane situations. Recognizing this was Tara's first step to healing and integration.

The journey of decoding emotions isn't always linear. It's like solving a jigsaw puzzle where pieces might not fit immediately, but with patience and persistence, a clearer picture emerges. Emotions are more than just fleeting feelings; they're signposts, guiding lights. By giving them the attention and understanding they deserve, we not only enhance our emotional well-being but also journey closer to our authentic selves. So the next time an emotion stirs within you, pause, reflect, and dive a little deeper. Who knows what treasures you might discover beneath the surface?

18

WOUNDING MAPPING: CHARTING THE SCARS OF THE SOUL

L ife is a vast canvas, painted with strokes of experiences—some vibrant, some muted, and some deeply shadowed. Much like an ancient tree stands tall bearing the markings of time, our souls, too, carry imprints from our journey. These imprints or wounds might seem like blemishes, areas we'd prefer to overlook or hide, but they are integral facets of who we are.

Have you ever considered, maybe even stopped to admire a tree's ability to transform every scar into a story? Every lightning strike, every broken branch, every groove, it tells a tale of resilience, of weathering storms, and emerging stronger. This tree doesn't wallow in the memories of past storms; instead, it stands tall, its scars a testament to its strength and resilience.

Similarly, every wound on our soul's canvas, be it a faint line or a deep gash, has a lesson to impart. Some teach resilience, some patience, some bring wisdom, while others instill compassion. These wounds might have originated from hurtful words, failed relation-ships, lost opportunities, or moments of self-doubt. But when we pause and reflect upon them, we realize that they have collectively sculpted our character, shaped our perceptions, and enriched our spirit.

Instead of viewing these wounds as marks of vulnerability or past pains, what if we looked at them as symbols of our growth, resilience, and strength? What if, instead of hiding them, we proudly displayed them, much like the tree, as stories of our journey, tales of our endurance? It's not the wounds that define us, but how we wear them.

———

UNDERSTANDING THE CONCEPT OF WOUNDS AND THEIR ORIGINS

Have you ever grazed your knee and noticed how, even after the pain has gone and the skin healed, a faint scar remains? Wounds of the soul function in much the same way. They're the emotional or psychological bruises, scratches, or deep cuts that events or people leave behind on our inner self. While they might not be visible to the naked eye, they can influence our behaviors, decisions, and reactions in profound ways.

These wounds aren't necessarily markers of grand tragedies. They don't always stem from significant traumas or dramatic heartbreaks. Sometimes, they're the result of subtle, seemingly trivial events—an offhand comment, a forgotten birthday, or a casual dismissal. The severity of the wound isn't determined by the event itself but by the impact it had on our psyche.

ORIGINS OF WOUNDS: THE ROOTS THAT RUN DEEP

Now, if we're delving into the concept of wounds, it's essential to understand where they come from. More often than not, the seeds are sown early, in the fertile grounds of childhood. A dismissive parent, an intimidating teacher, or a domineering sibling—any of these can be the source. But childhood isn't the only breeding ground. Relationships in our teenage years and adulthood, work environments, societal expectations, or even seemingly inconsequential daily interactions can all contribute.

There's also a fascinating, albeit somber, concept of ancestral traumas—wounds passed down through generations. This isn't about genetics but rather about learned behaviors and patterns. If a grandparent or parent experienced significant trauma and never processed or healed from it, they might unintentionally pass on the related behaviors, fears, or anxieties.

LISA'S TALE OF INVISIBLE CHAINS

To truly grasp the essence of wounds and their origins, let's consider Lisa's story. Lisa was a confident woman, successful in her professional life, and loved by her friends. Yet, there was this unexplainable unease she felt around authoritative figures. Be it her boss, a traffic cop, or even a stern-looking security guard at a concert—her heart would race, her palms would get sweaty, and an inexplicable anxiety would grip her.

Upon introspection and some guided reflection, Lisa traced this anxiety back to her primary school days. There was Ms. Thompson —a strict, no-nonsense teacher with a penchant for sharp rebukes. One day, after Lisa failed to complete her homework, Ms. Thompson berated her in front of the entire class. The event, while seemingly minor, left a deep scar on young Lisa's psyche. Even though years had passed, and Ms. Thompson was probably retired somewhere sipping on chamomile tea, the wound she inflicted remained, influencing Lisa's reactions in ways she couldn't fathom.

Through understanding and acknowledging the origin of her wound, Lisa was able to embark on her healing journey. But her story serves as a gentle reminder—sometimes, the chains that hold us aren't forged from steel but from memories, experiences, and unhealed wounds.

HOW TO MAP OUT YOUR WOUNDS

Mapping out our wounds is like embarking on an archaeological dig within our psyche. We delve deep, sift through layers, and uncover artifacts of our past—both pleasant and painful. This exercise isn't merely a trip down memory lane but a systematic excavation to understand our inner landscape better. Here's a step-by-step guide to help you chart out your emotional injuries:

1. Setting the Scene: The Sanctuary of Silence

Before we venture into the recesses of our memories, it's crucial to find the right environment. Locate a quiet corner in your home, maybe by a window or in a room where you feel most at ease. Ensure it's free of distractions—turn off the phone, keep away digital devices, and inform others, if any, not to disturb you for a while. Have a journal and a pen ready. If it helps, light a candle or play some soft, instrumental music in the background.

2. The Timeline Technique: Walking Down Memory Lane

Start at the very beginning. Think of your earliest memories—perhaps it's a scent, a toy, a person, or an incident. As you traverse through your timeline, move from early childhood to school days, teenage years, early adulthood, and so on.

Remember, this journey isn't about recalling every single event but focusing on moments, people, or situations that evoked strong emotions. Did a particular birthday stand out? Was there an incident in school that still makes your heart race?

3. Penning Down the Pivotal Points

As memories flood in, make sure you capture them in your journal. Note down each significant event or person and jot down the associated feelings. Was there heartache, joy, betrayal, pride? Be as descriptive as possible. If a specific incident made you feel "a swirling mix of anger and embarrassment," write it down just so.

4. The Color-Code Concept

This is where the artistic element comes in. Arm yourself with colored pens or highlighters. Assign a color to each emotion—maybe blue for sadness, red for anger, green for jealousy, and yellow for joy. Go through your journal and color-code each event or memory based on the dominant emotion it evoked. Over time, as you flip through your journal, you'll have a vibrant visual representation of your emotional journey.

5. Guided Imagery: The Book of Your Life

Close your eyes and imagine your life as a sprawling novel. Each chapter is a phase, an era of your life. Visualize flipping through its pages or even better, flick through your real pages that you've collared. Some chapters might be light and breezy, filled with sketches of sunny days and laughter. Others might be stormy, with illustrations of thunderclouds and rain.

Which events stand out the most? Who are the central characters in each chapter, and what roles did they play? What emotions arise as you 'read' your story? Remember, every book has its highs and lows, and it's the combination that makes it a gripping read. Your life is no different. Embrace each chapter, for they have made you the unique individual you are today.

This exercise can be both enlightening and emotionally taxing. If you feel overwhelmed at any point, it's okay to take a break, breathe, and come back to it later. Remember, the goal is healing and under-standing, not additional distress. Take your time and travel at a pace that feels comfortable for you.

ANALYZING AND REFLECTING ON MAPPED WOUNDS

So, you've mapped out your wounds. Pages filled with colored anno-tations, representing a myriad of emotions from various stages of your life. This isn't just a diary; it's a rich tapestry of your emotional journey. But the exploration doesn't end here. Now, it's time to delve deeper, to analyze and reflect upon these marked memories.

1. Deciphering the Dominant Hues

With your journal in hand, start by flipping through the pages. Notice the colors that seem most dominant. Are there clusters of blue denoting sadness or patches of red signaling anger?

Do you find that specific periods in your life were dominated by a particular emotion? Why do you think that is?

2. Recognizing Repetitive Patterns

As you continue your introspection, try to identify recurring themes or patterns. Maybe you've encountered feelings of rejection repeat-edly, be it from peers, family, or romantic relationships. Or perhaps there's a streak of yellow, indicating joyous occasions that revolved around a particular hobby or passion.

Consider Sophia, who kept noticing shades of green (representing jealousy) throughout her journal. On reflection, she realized her envy often stemmed from comparing her journey to others. Recognizing this pattern, she started working on cultivating self-love and gratitude for her unique path.

3. The Art of Reframing

Instead of dwelling on these wounds with a sense of melancholy, challenge yourself to reframe them. Yes, they were moments of pain, but they also added layers to your persona, depth to your character.

For each significant wound, write down a positive trait or lesson it fostered. Maybe a heartbreak taught you the importance of self-worth, or constant criticism from a parent instilled in you a drive to excel.

4. Mining the Silver Linings

For every dark cloud in our lives, there's invariably a silver lining, even if it's not immediately evident. Dive into each wound, no matter how painful, and seek that glint of positivity. Did a betrayal lead you to a tighter, more trustworthy circle of friends? Did an incident of public embarrassment eventually boost your self-confidence as you realized that everyone makes mistakes and life goes on?

I didn't make it into my dream university. However, the college I attended introduced me to lifelong friends and certain events and people who changed my career trajectory. Looking back, I now see that rejection as a redirection to a path I hadn't envisioned but now wouldn't change for the world. The path that led to this book, in fact.

Engaging in such reflective exercises isn't merely about introspection; it's also about transformation. By analyzing and understanding our wounds, we're better equipped to heal them and harness their lessons. Remember, every wound carries wisdom; every scar has a story. Embrace them, learn from them, and let them guide you towards a more enlightened self.

19

SELF-REFLECTION
WORKBOOK/JOURNAL SECTION

Before we venture into these pages, let's take a moment. Every blank space in this workbook is an invitation, not an obligation. It's a portal to your past, present, and future, but only if you wish to step through. Approach each prompt with an open heart and a gentle spirit, knowing that each word you write is a step closer to understanding and embracing your full self.

Foundation

When you think of your childhood, what is the first memory that comes to mind?

What emotions are tied to this memory?

Why do you think this particular recollection surfaced first?

Relationships

Which of your relationships have shaped you the most and why?

How have the dynamics of this relationship evolved over time?

In what ways has it influenced your current relationships?

Hidden Desires

What's something you've always wanted to do but haven't yet?

What's holding you back from pursuing this desire?

How would fulfilling this change your perception of yourself?

Challenges

What's the challenge you faced that's had the biggest impact on your life trajectory?

How did you grow from this experience?

What resources (internal or external) did you draw upon to navigate it?

Shadows and Fears

What's your most secret fear?

From where do you think this fear originated?

How does it influence your choices and reactions?

Dreams and Aspirations

If you had all the resources and time in the world, what would you want to do?

What does this aspiration reveal about your values and passions?

Is there a small step you can take today towards this dream?

Personal Growth

What's a stage in your life that you feel you've come a long way from in terms of personal growth?

Recognize and honor the growth that's brought you to this point.

What were the pivotal moments or decisions that propelled you forward?

Closure

Having traveled through these pages, you've unveiled fragments of your psyche, your desires, fears, and dreams. Take a moment to acknowledge the bravery it takes to confront these aspects of oneself. Let this workbook serve as a living document, one you can revisit, add to, or revise as you continue on your journey of self-discovery.

20

INNER CHILD AFFIRMATIONS WORKBOOK/JOURNAL SECTION

D eep within us, there's a child. This isn't a metaphorical child, but the very essence of who we were in our formative years. Every joy, pain, hope, and fear from those times still resides within us. This workbook/journal is dedicated to that child, helping you reconnect, heal, and nurture that precious part of yourself.

Understanding the Inner Child

Close your eyes and picture yourself as a child. What are you doing? Where are you? How do you feel?

This mental image is a window into your inner child's world. What does this snapshot tell you about your younger self's needs, desires, and emotions?

Moments with the Inner Child

Recall a specific moment from your childhood where you felt particularly vulnerable or misunderstood.

How does this memory make your adult self feel now? What would you tell this younger version of yourself knowing what you know today?

Crafting Affirmations

Think of the emotions or situations that often troubled your younger self. Now, craft an affirmation that directly addresses that pain or fear. Example: If you often felt ignored, your affirmation might be, "My voice is valuable and deserves to be heard."

Space for Your Affirmations:

Daily Practices for Your Inner Child

Dedicate a few minutes each day to visualize holding or comforting your younger self.

Create a small corner or space in your home filled with items that your younger self would have loved.

At the end of each day, write a small note or letter to your inner child. It could be words of comfort, understanding, or just sharing your day.

Write down one activity you'll commit to for the next week to nurture your inner child:

Inner Child Affirmation Log

Every morning or evening, write down an affirmation dedicated to your inner child. Notice how your relationship with these affirmations evolves over time.

Date: _____
Affirmation: _____

Date: _____
Affirmation: _____

Date: _____
Affirmation: _____

Date: _____
Affirmation: _____

Date: _____
Affirmation: _____

Date: _____
Affirmation: _____

Date: _____
Affirmation: _____

Date: _____
Affirmation: _____

Date: _____
Affirmation: _____

Date: _____
Affirmation: _____

Date: _____
Affirmation: _____

Date: _____
Affirmation: _____

Date: _____
Affirmation: _____

Date: _____
Affirmation: _____

Date: _____
Affirmation: _____

Date: _____
Affirmation: _____

Date: _____
Affirmation: _____

Date: _____
Affirmation: _____

Date: _____
Affirmation: _____

Date: _____
Affirmation: _____

Moments of Reconnection

Describe a recent situation where you felt a strong connection to your inner child. What triggered this connection? How did you respond?

How can you create more of these reconnection moments? Are there specific triggers you can identify that typically evoke your inner child?

Celebration of the Inner Child

Draw, paint, or doodle something that your inner child would love. Let this be a free space to express without judgment.

How did it feel to engage in this activity? Were there any memories or emotions that surfaced?

Nurturing your inner child is a journey of love, patience, and understanding. With every affirmation, every moment of reconnection, you're not just healing the child within but also creating a harmonious relationship with the entirety of who you are.

21

GRATITUDE LIST
WORKBOOK/JOURNAL SECTION

At the heart of our very existence is the ability to feel and express gratitude. Gratitude is more than just saying "thank you." It's a profound recognition of the good in our lives—even during challenging times. This workbook/journal invites you to explore the transformative power of gratitude in your healing journey.

The Healing Power of Gratitude

Think of a time when expressing or feeling gratitude brought a positive change in your perspective, mood, or overall day.

What was the situation? How did gratitude shift your emotional state or perspective?

The Science Behind Gratitude

Studies have shown that practicing gratitude can enhance our mood, reduce stress, and improve overall well-being. Our brains are wired to focus on negative stimuli, but consistent gratitude practices can rewire them for positivity.

Reflect on a period in your life when you were facing challenges. Can you find three things from that time you're grateful for?

Setting Up Your Gratitude Journal

Choose a specific time each day to jot down what you're grateful for.

Instead of broad statements, delve into specifics. Instead of "I'm grateful for my family," you might write, "I'm grateful for the way my sister made me laugh today."

As you write, take a moment to genuinely feel the gratitude.

Write down five things you're grateful for today. Dive into the specifics!

Gratitude Beyond the Obvious

Think of something or someone you have a challenging relationship with. Can you find an aspect of this challenge to be grateful for? Maybe it's a lesson learned or personal growth experienced.

How does focusing on gratitude change your perspective on this challenge?

Daily Gratitude Log

Each day, jot down at least three things you're grateful for. Over time, you'll see patterns and shifts in your perspective.

Date: _____
1. _____
2. _____
3. _____

Date: _____
1. _____
2. _____
3. _____

Date: _____
1. _____
2. _____
3. _____

Date: _____
1. _____
2. _____
3. _____

Date: _____
1. _____
2. _____
3. _____

Date: _____
1. _____
2. _____

3. _____

Date: _____
1. _____
2. _____
3. _____

Date: _____
1. _____
2. _____
3. _____

Reflecting on Your Gratitude Journey

Look back over the past entries. Do you notice any recurring themes or patterns?

How has this daily practice impacted your mood, perspective, or overall well-being?

Gratitude in Action

Choose one act of gratitude you can extend to someone else today. It could be a heartfelt thank you note, a small gift, or simply expressing appreciation.

How did it feel to express gratitude in this manner? How was your gesture received?

Closure

Gratitude isn't just a feeling—it's a lifestyle. The more we practice it, the more we realize how much goodness surrounds us. Even on the cloudy days, there's always a silver lining, always something to be grateful for. This journey of gratitude is transformative, bringing light, love, and healing to the forefront of our lives.

22

A LETTER TO YOUR PAST SELF WORKBOOK/JOURNAL SECTION

E very chapter in our life's story (or this book) holds its own significance. By revisiting these pages, we embark on a journey of reflection and rediscovery. Writing a letter to your past self bridges the distance between who you were and who you've become. It's a therapeutic dance of memories and moments, blending self-awareness, self-compassion, and personal growth into a waltz of words.

As we commence this introspective journey, let's light the path. Delve deep into your memories and consider those defining instances that sculpted you.

Setting the Mood

Finding Solitude: *Choose a quiet space, free from distractions.*

Breathing Deeply: *Take a few deep breaths, grounding yourself in the present moment.*

Visualizing: *Close your eyes and picture your past self. Imagine their fears, hopes, joys, and sorrows.*

Jot down three significant moments from your past that resonate strongly in your heart and mind. As you reflect, remember that these moments can range from grand events to subtle shifts.

Remember, there's no "right" or "wrong" memory. Trust your intuition; it often leads us to insights we might have overlooked.

Now, write down three words that currently describe your past self.

Guided Prompts for Your Letter

As you write, be compassionate, understanding, and non-judgmental. This is a safe space.

Prompts:

1. *Start by describing a vivid memory you share with your past self.*
2. *Express gratitude for the lessons learned and strength garnered.*
3. *Share words of comfort for the challenges faced.*
4. *Convey the hope and beauty of the future that awaits.*
5. **Guided Head Start:** *"Dear [Your Name], I remember when..."*

Letter space (more on next page)

Letter space

Reflecting on the Experience

After finishing the letter, how do you feel? Is there a sense of lightness, closure, or newfound understanding?

Share your thoughts and emotions after revisiting those pivotal moments with your past self.

Gaining Closure

Find a serene spot. Read your letter aloud to yourself. Feel the words, absorb their significance, and let them resonate within.

How has this exercise helped you see your growth? Are there any feelings or situations you've found closure with through this letter?

THE MIRROR

By reaching back and connecting with our past, we embrace the entirety of our journey. Every challenge, every joy, every tear, and every laugh has shaped us. By honoring our past self, we pave the way for a more understanding, compassionate, and whole future self.

The mirror: a fixture in our daily lives, commonly used to ensure our outward appearance meets societal expectations. But what if, beyond its apparent utility, it could be a gateway to the profound depths of our being? Enter the practice of mirror gazing. An ancient ritual, this exercise pushes past the surface to help us traverse the labyrinthine corridors of our psyche. It's not just about seeing our reflection; it's about acknowledging, understanding, and accepting the person staring back.

Throughout history, mirrors have held a mystical allure. They've been used in various cultures for divination, self-reflection, and spiritual practices. From ancient Egyptian rituals to modern-day psychological therapies, mirror gazing has been both a tool for predicting the future and understanding the self.

THE POWER OF SELF-REFLECTION

When we intentionally connect with our reflection, we're confronted with raw emotions, hidden fears, and suppressed desires. This connection can:

- **Reveal Authenticity:** Helps us distinguish between the masks we wear and our true selves.
- **Prompt Introspection:** Encourages us to question why certain emotions or memories arise.
- **Facilitate Healing:** By acknowledging our feelings, we can begin the journey to wholeness.

The Journey Within Through Mirror Gazing

Mirror gazing isn't about vanity or self-obsession; it's a profound and intentional act of diving into the depths of one's soul. By looking beyond the superficial, you're afforded an intimate rendezvous with the person you've been, are, and are becoming.

Here are the main parts of mirror gazing:

1. Enhanced Self-awareness:

What It Is: Recognizing the intricacies of our ever-evolving selves. Understanding our emotions, desires, fears, and aspirations.

In Practice: As you gaze, you may notice subtle facial reactions to thoughts, or even an emotional response to memories. These are windows into understanding oneself.

Real-life Glimpse: Mark, during his first session of mirror gazing, observed a twitch in his eyebrow whenever he thought of his childhood. This twitch was a gateway to understanding his unresolved feelings about his past.

2. Emotional Release:

What It Is: The liberation of feelings that might have been buried under the day-to-day hustle. It's a cathartic experience.

In Practice: Tears, laughter, or even a serene sense of peace – any of these might manifest. Welcome them all.

Personal Reflection: Sarah, while gazing, found herself shedding tears. On introspection, she realized they were tears of gratitude for the hurdles she'd overcome, turning her pain into strength.

3. Intuitive Boost:

What It Is: Strengthening that inner voice, the gut feeling, the sixth sense. Tapping into an inherent wisdom that often gets overshadowed by external noise.

In Practice: With consistent mirror gazing, you may find your decisions becoming more aligned with your true desires and values. You'll learn to trust yourself more.

Inspiring Tale: Alex, after months of practice, began noticing a heightened sense of intuition. It was as if the mirror had fine-tuned his internal compass, guiding him in personal and professional decisions.

THE SACRED STEPS TO SELF-REFLECTION THROUGH MIRROR GAZING

1. Setting the Ambience:

Just as a plant requires the right environment to grow, your introspective journey with mirror gazing needs the appropriate setting.

Consider lighting a candle or two. The soft flicker can create a calming atmosphere and provide just the right amount of light.

2. Perfect Positioning:

Your physical comfort is crucial. An improper position can distract from the experience.

Ensure your back is supported. You might want to use cushions or backrests.

3. Breathing: The Anchor:

Your breath acts as a bridge between the external world and your inner self. It grounds and prepares you for the journey ahead.

Take three deep breaths – inhale for 4 counts, hold for 4 counts, exhale for 4 counts.

4. Gaze Beyond the Surface:

This isn't about the physicality but the soul. It's a gateway to deeper understanding.

Imagine your eyes as two mystical pools, each holding stories, memories, and wisdom. Dive into them.

5. Making the Connection:

This step is akin to wading through a stream filled with leaves (your fleeting thoughts). The aim isn't to remove the leaves but to find the flow.

Every time a thought distracts you, imagine it as a leaf floating away, allowing you to focus on the clear water beneath.

6. Setting a Timer:

While there's no strict duration, starting small ensures you don't get overwhelmed.

As your practice deepens, you may lose track of time. Set a gentle alarm or use a meditation app to signal the end of the session.

REFLECT & JOURNAL SECTION:

Post your gazing session, take a moment to jot down any insights, feelings, or visions that emerged during the exercise.

Was there a predominant emotion or memory that surfaced?

Did you observe any physical sensations during the exercise?

How did you feel post the session, and what did you learn about yourself?

"By looking deeply into the mirror of our soul, we find the reflection of the universe."

CONCLUSION

If there's one thing I hope you take away from this deep dive into the world of shadows, it's that there's no journey more rewarding than the one leading to your own heart. Venturing into the depths of your psyche, while undoubtedly challenging, is the most profound act of self-love. Why? Because you're saying, "I am worth knowing. All of me."

Over time, even the largest and most beautiful gardens get overshadowed by large trees, leading to the growth of weeds and the wilting of flowers. But with every weed you pull out, with every branch you trim, light begins to seep in. The garden rejuvenates. That garden is you.

By integrating your shadows, not only do you release blocked energies and heal past wounds, but you also make space for new, vibrant energies to take root. The past triggers that once held you captive lose their grip, making way for fresh experiences and learnings.

Throughout this book, I've made it clear that this is a journey. I didn't use that term lightly. Like any meaningful journey, it's filled with mountains and valleys, clear days, and stormy nights. And just like any traveler will tell you, it's not about the destination but the journey itself. The insights you gain, the emotions you feel, and the growth you experience—these are the markers of your trail.

If you ever feel overwhelmed, take a step back. Breathe. Remember why you embarked on this path. Wasn't it to understand yourself better? To love yourself more fully? To heal the child within? Every challenge you face and every shadow you integrate is a testament to your strength and commitment to self-growth.

In the words of the great Carl Jung, "One does not become enlightened by imagining figures of light, but by making the darkness conscious." Your shadows aren't adversaries; they're parts of you, waiting to be acknowledged, understood, and loved.

Don't let this conclusion be the end. Because, dear reader, every layer you peel back reveals a more authentic, more vibrant you.

Books close. Stories end. But your journey? It's just getting started.

Embrace it. Celebrate it. Grow through it.

REFERENCE LIST

Church, D., Hawk, C., Brooks, A.J., Toukolehto, O., Wren, M., Dinter, I. and Stein, P. (2013). Psychological Trauma Symptom Improvement in Veterans Using Emotional Freedom Techniques. *Journal of Nervous & Mental Disease*, 201(2), pp.153–160. doi:https://doi.org/10.1097/nmd.0b013e31827f6351.

Gallant, S.N. (2016). Mindfulness meditation practice and executive functioning: Breaking down the benefit. *Consciousness and Cognition*, 40, pp.116–130. doi:https://doi.org/10.1016/j.concog.2016.01.005.

Freud, S., Strachey, J., Tyson, A. and Richards, A. (1976). *The interpretation of dreams / The present volume edited by Angela Richards.* Harmondsworth: Penguin.

Huntington, C. (n.d.). *Shadow Work: Definition, Examples, & Prompts.* [online] The Berkeley Well-Being Institute. Available at: https://www.berkeleywellbeing.com/shadow-work.html [Accessed 26 Jul. 2023].

Jung, C. and Jung, C.G. (2008). *The Concept of the Collective Unconscious.* [online] Available at: http://www.bahaistudies.net/asma/The-Concept-of-the-Collective-Unconscious.pdf.

Jung, C.G. (2012). *Psychology of the Unconscious.* Courier Corporation.

Petriglieri, G. and Stein, M. (2012). The Unwanted Self: Projective Identification in Leaders' Identity Work. *Organization Studies*, 33(9), pp.1217–1235. doi:https://doi.org/10.1177/0170840612448158.

Practical Psychology. (2020). *Carl Jung Biography | Psychologists.* [online] Available at: https://practicalpsychology.com/carl-jung/ [Accessed 23 July. 2023].

Simmons, M. (2023). Inner Work Community: Shadow Work as Spiritual Formation. *Doctor of Leadership.* [online] Available at: https://digitalcommons.georgefox.edu/dld/9/ [Accessed 26 Jul. 2023].

Thurmond, D. (2012). The Influence of Carl Jung's Archetype of the Shadow On Early 20th Century Literature. *Master of Liberal Studies Theses.* [online] Available at: https://scholarship.rollins.edu/mls/32/.

Wilber, K. (2008). *Integral life practice : a 21st-century blueprint for physical health, emotional balance, mental clarity, and spiritual awakening.* Boston Integral Books.